RUTH BADER GINSBURG

WOMEN of ACHIEVEMENT

RUTH BADER GINSBURG

Linda Bayer, Ph.D.

CHELSEA HOUSE PUBLISHERS
PHILADELPHIA

Dedication: The author wishes to dedicate this book to her niece Rose Bess Bayer, who appears to be following in the footsteps of her father, Aaron Bayer, deputy attorney general for the state of Connecticut, and her mother, Dr. Laurie Bayer, a dedicated pediatrician. May Rose and her twin brothers, Philip and Abraham, be among the first generation during which gender and religious discrimination no longer block the progress of gifted, creative youngsters. Perhaps Rose will follow Ruth Bader Ginsburg to the Supreme Court or to wherever her bright lights may take her.

Cover Photo: AP/Wide World Photos

Frontis: In 1993, Justice Ruth Bader Ginsburg took her seat on the Supreme Court as the second woman in U.S. history to become a justice on the nation's highest court.

PRODUCED BY 21st Century Publishing and Communications, Inc., New York, NY
CONTRIBUTING EDITOR Elaine Andrews

Chelsea House Publishers
EDITOR IN CHIEF Stephen Reginald
PRODUCTION MANAGER Pamela Loos
ART DIRECTOR Sara Davis
DIRECTOR OF PHOTOGRAPHY Judy L. Hasday
MANAGING EDITOR James D. Gallagher
SENIOR PRODUCTION EDITOR LeeAnne Gelletly
COVER DESIGNER Keith Trego

The Chelsea House World Wide Web address is
http://www.chelseahouse.com

First Printing
1 3 5 7 9 8 6 4 2

Library of Congress Cataloging-in-Publication Data

Bayer, Linda N.
Ruth Bader Ginsburg / Linda Bayer.
    p.   cm. — (Women of achievement)
Includes bibliographical references and index.
Summary: Presents the life and accomplishments of the second woman justice named to the United States Supreme Court.

ISBN 0-7910-5287-7 (hc) — ISBN 0-7910-5288-5 (pb)

1. Ginsburg, Ruth Bader—Juvenile literature. 2. Judges—United States—Biography—Juvenile literature. 3. United States. Supreme Court—Biography—Juvenile literature. [1. Ginsburg, Ruth Bader. 2. Judges. 3. United States. Supreme Court—Biography. 4. Women—Biography.] I. Title. II. Series.

KF8745.G56 B39 2000
347.73'3534—dc21   99-055998
[B]   CIP
                                                                               AC

CONTENTS

WOMEN of ACHIEVEMENT

Jane Addams
SOCIAL WORKER

Madeleine Albright
STATESWOMAN

Marian Anderson
SINGER

Susan B. Anthony
WOMAN SUFFRAGIST

Clara Barton
AMERICAN RED CROSS FOUNDER

Margaret Bourke-White
PHOTOGRAPHER

Rachel Carson
BIOLOGIST AND AUTHOR

Cher
SINGER AND ACTRESS

Hillary Rodham Clinton
FIRST LADY AND ATTORNEY

Katie Couric
JOURNALIST

Diana, Princess of Wales
HUMANITARIAN

Emily Dickinson
POET

Elizabeth Dole
POLITICIAN

Amelia Earhart
AVIATOR

Gloria Estefan
SINGER

Jodie Foster
ACTRESS AND DIRECTOR

Betty Friedan
FEMINIST

Althea Gibson
TENNIS CHAMPION

Ruth Bader Ginsburg
SUPREME COURT JUSTICE

Helen Hayes
ACTRESS

Katharine Hepburn
ACTRESS

Mahalia Jackson
GOSPEL SINGER

Helen Keller
HUMANITARIAN

**Ann Landers/
Abigail Van Buren**
COLUMNISTS

Barbara McClintock
BIOLOGIST

Margaret Mead
ANTHROPOLOGIST

Edna St. Vincent Millay
POET

Julia Morgan
ARCHITECT

Toni Morrison
AUTHOR

Grandma Moses
PAINTER

Lucretia Mott
WOMAN SUFFRAGIST

Sandra Day O'Connor
SUPREME COURT JUSTICE

Rosie O'Donnell
ENTERTAINER AND COMEDIAN

Georgia O'Keeffe
PAINTER

Eleanor Roosevelt
DIPLOMAT AND HUMANITARIAN

Wilma Rudolph
CHAMPION ATHLETE

Elizabeth Cady Stanton
WOMAN SUFFRAGIST

Harriet Beecher Stowe
AUTHOR AND ABOLITIONIST

Barbra Streisand
ENTERTAINER

Elizabeth Taylor
ACTRESS AND ACTIVIST

Mother Teresa
HUMANITARIAN AND
RELIGIOUS LEADER

Barbara Walters
JOURNALIST

Edith Wharton
AUTHOR

Phillis Wheatley
POET

Oprah Winfrey
ENTERTAINER

Babe Didrikson Zaharias
CHAMPION ATHLETE

"REMEMBER THE LADIES"

MATINA S. HORNER

"Remember the Ladies." That is what Abigail Adams wrote to her husband John, then a delegate to the Continental Congress, as the Founding Fathers met in Philadelphia to form a new nation in March of 1776. "Be more generous and favorable to them than your ancestors. Do not put such unlimited power in the hands of the Husbands. If particular care and attention is not paid to the Ladies," Abigail Adams warned, "we are determined to foment a Rebellion, and will not hold ourselves bound by any Laws in which we have no voice, or Representation."

The words of Abigail Adams, one of the earliest American advocates of women's rights, were prophetic. Because when we have not "remembered the ladies," they have, by their words and deeds, reminded us so forcefully of the omission that we cannot fail to remember them. For the history of American women is as interesting and varied as the history of our nation as a whole. American women have played an integral part in founding, settling, and building our country. Some we remember as remarkable women who—against great odds—achieved distinction in the public arena: Anne Hutchinson, who in the 17th century became a charismatic religious leader; Phillis Wheatley, an 18th-century black slave who became a poet; Susan B. Anthony, whose name is synonymous with the 19th-century women's rights movement, and who led the struggle to enfranchise women; and in the 20th century, Amelia Earhart, the first woman to cross the Atlantic Ocean by air.

These extraordinary women certainly merit our admiration, but other women, "common women," many of them all but forgotten, should also be recognized for their contributions to American thought and culture. Women have been community builders; they have founded schools and formed voluntary associations to help those in need; they have assumed the major responsibility for rearing children, passing on from one generation to the next the values that keep a culture alive. These and innumerable other contributions, once ignored, are now being recognized by scholars, students, and the public. It is exciting and gratifying that a part of our history that was hardly acknowledged a few generations ago is now being studied and brought to light.

In recent decades, the field of women's history has grown from obscurity to a politically controversial splinter movement to academic respectability, in many cases mainstreamed into such traditional disciplines as history, economics, and psychology. Scholars of women, both female and male, have organized research centers at such prestigious institutions as Wellesley College, Stanford University, and the University of California. Other notable centers for women's studies are the Center for the American Woman and Politics at the Eagleton Institute of Politics at Rutgers University; the Henry A. Murray Research Center for the Study of Lives, at Radcliffe College; and the Women's Research and Education Institute, the research arm of the Congressional Caucus on Women's Issues. Other scholars and public figures have established archives and libraries, such as the Schlesinger Library on the History of Women in America, at Radcliffe College, and the Sophia Smith Collection, at Smith College, to collect and preserve the written and tangible legacies of women.

From the initial donation of the Women's Rights Collection in 1943, the Schlesinger Library grew to encompass vast collections documenting the manifold accomplishments of American women. Simultaneously, the women's movement in general and the academic discipline of women's studies in particular also began with a narrow definition and gradually expanded their mandate. Early causes, such as woman suffrage and social reform, abolition, and organized labor were joined by newer concerns, such as the history of women in business and the professions and in politics and government; the study of the family; and social issues such as health policy and education.

Women, as historian Arthur M. Schlesinger, jr., once pointed out, "have constituted the most spectacular casualty of traditional history. They have made up at least half the human race, but you could never tell that by looking at the books historians write." The new breed of historians is remedying that omission. They have written books about immigrant women and about working-class women who struggled for survival in cities and about black women who met the challenges of life in rural areas. They are telling the stories of women who, despite the barriers of tradition and economics, became lawyers and doctors and public figures.

The women's studies movement has also led scholars to question traditional interpretations of their respective disciplines. For example, the study of war has traditionally been an exercise in military and political analysis, an examination of strategies planned and executed by men. But scholars of women's history have pointed out that wars have also been periods of tremendous change and even opportunity for women, because the very absence of men on the home front enabled them to expand their educational, economic, and professional activities and to assume leadership in their homes.

The early scholars of women's history showed a unique brand of courage in choosing to investigate new subjects and take new approaches to old ones. Often, like their subjects, they endured criticism and even ostracism by their academic colleagues. But their efforts have unquestionably been worthwhile, because with the publication of each new study and book another piece of the historical patchwork is sewn into place, revealing an increasingly comprehensive picture of the role of women in our rich and varied history.

Such books on groups of women are essential, but books that focus on the lives of individuals are equally indispensable. Biographies can be inspirational, offering their readers the example of people with vision who have looked outside themselves for their goals and have often struggled against great obstacles to achieve them. Marian Anderson, for instance, had to overcome racial bigotry in order to perfect her art and perform as a concert singer. Isadora Duncan defied the rules of classical dance to find true artistic freedom. Jane Addams had to break down society's notions of the proper role for women in order to create new social situations, notably the settlement house. All of these women had to come to terms both with themselves and with the world in which they lived. Only then could they move ahead as pioneers in their chosen callings.

Biography can inspire not only by adulation but also by realism. It helps us to see not only the qualities in others that we hope to emulate, but also, perhaps, the weaknesses that made them "human." By helping us identify with the subject on a more personal level they help us feel that we, too, can achieve such goals. We read about Eleanor Roosevelt, for instance, who occupied a unique and seemingly enviable position as the wife of the president. Yet we can sympathize with her inner dilemma; an inherently shy woman, she had to force herself to live a most public life in order to use her position to benefit others. We may not be able to imagine ourselves having the immense poetic talent of Emily Dickinson, but from her story we can understand the challenges faced by a creative woman who was expected to fulfill many family responsibilities. And though few of us will ever reach the level of athletic accomplishment displayed by Wilma Rudolph or Babe Zaharias, we can still appreciate their spirit, their overwhelming will to excel.

A biography is a multifaceted lens. It is first of all a magnification, the intimate examination of one particular life. But at the same time, it is a wide-angle lens, informing us about the world in which the subject lived. We come away from reading about one life knowing more about the social, political, and economic fabric of the time. It is for this reason, perhaps, that the great New England essayist Ralph Waldo Emerson wrote in 1841, "There is properly no history: only biography." And it is also why biography, and particularly women's biography, will continue to fascinate writers and readers alike.

With President Bill Clinton at her side, Ruth Bader Ginsburg accepts her nomination to the Supreme Court. Her appointment was the culmination of a long and distinguished career as lawyer, judge, and advocate for equal justice for all Americans.

1

THE JOURNEY BEGINS

Monday, June 14, 1993, was a beautiful day in the Rose Garden of the White House. President Bill Clinton was holding a press conference to announce his nominee for the Supreme Court of the United States. The candidate and her proud family gathered with friends, members of Congress, and the media to hear the president name his choice for the post of 107th justice of the Court. Clinton had chosen Ruth Bader Ginsburg, only the second woman ever to be nominated to the highest court in the nation.

In his introduction, President Clinton praised Ginsburg's abilities and experience, noting especially her role as a trailblazer for women's rights. "Having experienced discrimination," he said, "she devoted the next 20 years of her career to fighting it and making this country a better place for our wives, our mothers, our sisters, and our daughters."

The petite, 60-year-old grandmother who stepped forward had for 13 years been a judge on the United States Court of Appeals for the District of Columbia Circuit. As she acknowledged the president's introduction, she praised the women's movement for helping to make it possible for women like her to reach such high positions. She remarked that her nomination "contributes to the end of the days when women, at least half the talent pool in our society, appear in places only as one-at-a-time performers."

Judge Ginsburg saved her final words for the first person who had shaped her life—her mother, who had died young. "I have a last thank-you," she said. "It is to my mother, Celia Amster Bader, the bravest and strongest person I have known, who was taken from me much too soon. I pray that I may be all that she would have been had she lived in an age when women could aspire and achieve, and daughters are cherished as much as sons."

President Clinton was moved to tears as he told the press that Judge Ginsburg "repeatedly stood for the individual, the person less well-off, the outsider in society, and has given those people greater hope by telling them they have a place in our legal system."

The road from Ruth's early childhood in Brooklyn, New York, to the Supreme Court was a long one. There were disappointments and hardship, but her intelligence, determination, and heart helped her triumph. Through her work in the courts and by her own example, Ruth Bader Ginsburg opened doors that for years had been shut by bias and prejudice against women and minorities.

On March 15, 1933, Celia and Nathan Bader of Belle Harbor, Queens (a borough of New York City), became the proud parents of their second daughter, Joan Ruth. A little more than two years later, the family moved to the Flatbush section of the borough of Brooklyn, where Joan Ruth Bader grew up. When she entered kindergarten, two other Joan Ruths were in the class, so Celia registered her daughter as Ruth Joan Bader.

Most of Ruth's friends called her "Kiki," a nickname bestowed on her by her sister, Marilyn, because

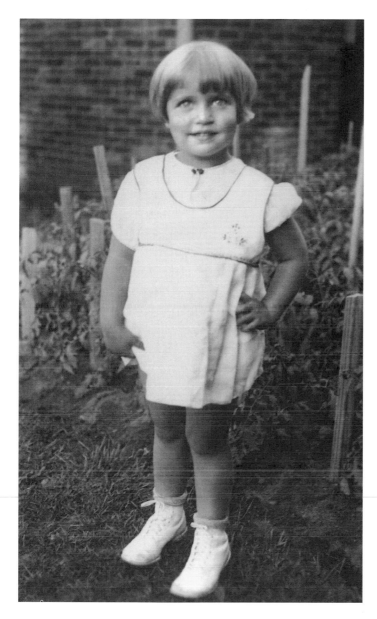

Two-year-old Ruth poses for a photo. As a little girl, Ruth was surrounded by a warm and loving family that encouraged her at an early age to work hard to achieve her goals.

on one occasion toddler Ruth had kicked her cousin Richard. Until Ruth was four years old, she and Richard Bader lived in the same household, which allowed Richard and Ruth's families to share household expenses. Later, the cousins lived close by in the same neighborhood. Only three months apart in age, the two were very close. One of Ruth's earliest memories is of playing ball with Richard—using a tomato for the ball.

The Bader family lived on the ground floor of a tidy two-story building in a middle-class neighborhood. Celia took care of the house and children, while Nathan worked in a shop making fur hats, coats, and muffs. Ruth's paternal grandparents lived a few blocks away, and the extended family celebrated holidays together. Like many Jews of their generation, Ruth's paternal and maternal grandparents had emigrated to the United States from Eastern Europe to escape persecution and find religious freedom and better economic opportunities. When Ruth was growing up, Flatbush was a community of hard-working Jewish, Irish, and Italian immigrant families who hoped to attain the American dream for their children.

Tragedy struck the Bader household when Ruth's sister, Marilyn, died of meningitis, a disease that infects the brain and spinal cord, at age eight. Ruth, only two at the time, does not really remember her sister. "I have some notebooks she wrote and photographs," Justice Ginsburg recounts. Perhaps as a result of this early loss, Ruth became extremely close to her parents. Nathan was a loving, doting father, whereas Celia was the disciplinarian who encouraged learning and achievement in her bright, blond-haired child.

Ruth's early years were also colored by the Great Depression of the 1930s in the United States, a decade during which millions of Americans suffered from unemployment and poverty. Ruth was also affected by stories of the Holocaust that occurred during World War II in Europe, when Nazi Germany annihilated six million Jews. She learned as a young girl the terrible results of anti-Semitism. Despite the shadow of the Depression and the Holocaust, Ruth enjoyed a childhood in which she was encouraged by her parents, as Justice Ginsburg later recalled, "to love

learning, care about people, and work hard" at whatever she wanted to accomplish.

Celia Bader instilled in her daughter a love of reading.
Some of Ruth's fondest memories are of accompany-
ing her mother to the public library off Kings Highway
in Brooklyn and poring over books together. And,
although Celia herself had begun working at age 15 so
that her eldest brother could attend college, she firmly
believed that girls should have the same opportunities as
boys. With this in mind, Celia began saving money for
Ruth's college fund.

In 1938, Ruth entered Public School 238, where
she soon proved her academic abilities. As editor of the
student publication *Highway Herald*, she wrote articles

*When Ruth was growing up
during the Great Depression,
large numbers of people were
unemployed. It was not
uncommon to see long lines
of people waiting to receive
free food distributed by public
and private organizations.*

This photograph of Ruth and her cousin Richard Bader was taken when Ruth was 10 years old. Ruth and Richard grew up together and were especially close.

about the history of the school, the local parents' association, and the roots of the U.S. judicial system. While in the eighth grade, Ruth composed an editorial called "Landmarks of Constitutional Freedom." The composition was, perhaps, an early indication of her future love of the law.

In the editorial, Ruth identified five great human rights documents—the Ten Commandments, England's Magna Carta, the Bill of Rights of England, the Declaration of Independence, and the charter of the United Nations. Ruth expressed a sense of history and the insight of someone much older. She explained how these documents shaped the history of the world by establishing ideas of human rights and standards of conduct.

Ruth also had literary gifts, which she expressed when Principal Dominic R. Hunt died suddenly not long before her graduation. He was remembered in the school paper for his "justice, tolerance, conscientiousness, hard work, and kindly, helpful spirit." Ruth added to this tribute by commemorating the beloved teacher and administrator with a poem. Reflecting the sense of loss that all the students felt, she penned "A Tribute to Mr. Hunt":

Never must we think of him as gone,
For never could that be.
He is off on a distant journey
Where the Almighty guards him constantly.
And though he is gone from our vision,
In all our hearts and minds
Forever in gold letters shall his name be enshrined.

While studying and writing for the school paper, Ruth still found time to enjoy reading. She loved to read about mythology—the legends of the gods, goddesses, and heroes of ancient Rome and Greece. She was especially fond of the stories of Pallas Athena, the beautiful Greek goddess of wisdom and art. The young reader also counted the children's classics *Winnie-the-Pooh*, *A Secret Garden*, and *Mary Poppins* among her favorites.

Ruth's reading included the adventures of the fictional young detective Nancy Drew, the teenager who solved cases through crackerjack investigations. Today, Justice Ginsburg recalls that she liked Nancy Drew "because she was smarter than her boyfriend."

Ruth's role models were women of accomplishment. For example, she admired the exploits of Amelia Earhart, the famous American aviator. Earhart made many record-breaking flights, including surpassing the women pilots' altitude record in 1922 and venturing

This is an undated photo of Amelia Earhart (1897– 1937). As one of the first female aviators to attempt an around-the-world flight, Earhart was one of the most renowned and daring women of her day.

solo across the Atlantic Ocean in 1932. She also joined Purdue University in Indiana as a career adviser to women and began her own charter airline. Earhart challenged gender barriers, influenced women's positions in the young aviation industry, and advocated self-reliance and equal rights for all women. Although Earhart later disappeared in 1937 during a flight over the Pacific Ocean, her success as an aviator and business-woman inspired countless women such as Ruth.

Young Ruth Bader's imagination soared as she read of the adventures of others, but her years at P.S. 238 were not solely devoted to books. One of her childhood friends maintains that Ruth was not "bookish" at all, despite her excellent grades and fondness for reading. In fact, Ruth was a well-rounded student. Among other activities, she participated in the eighth-grade devil-ball tournament in which her team was victorious. She displayed a certain acting ability when she played a princess denied her true love in a student production of *The King's Cream Puffs*, a romantic drama. She also provided the music for a student production of *The Trial of March*, in which the inclement month was accused of being "cruel and reckless." Outside school, Ruth was something of a tomboy. She belonged to a group that often climbed onto rooftops around her home and flung stones at groups of other girls and boys from the neighborhood.

On June 24, 1946, Ruth Bader graduated from P.S. 238 and was honored with a scholarship for outstanding achievement and service to the school. After the school orchestra, to which Ruth belonged, played "Land of Hope and Glory" as well as Beethoven's Fifth Symphony, she and classmate Stella Berg delivered the valedictory speech.

Ruth Bader was ready to embark on the next step in her education. She looked forward to entering James Madison High School the following autumn. Her future was full of promise and hope.

When Ruth was a counselor at her summer camp, she served as the "camper rabbi." Already an accomplished speaker, Ruth is shown here, at the age of 15, delivering a sermon to fellow campers.

2

A HOPEFUL FUTURE

A quiet, modest, highly intelligent teenager, Ruth was popular among her classmates at James Madison High School in Brooklyn. A friend and classmate, Ann Burkhardt Kittner, recalls clearly, "She had piercing blue eyes and a certain magnetism that drew people to her." Ruth's modesty was also remembered by a close high school friend, Harryette Gordon Helsel: "Ruth wouldn't speak unless she had something to say. She was always thinking. You might not even have realized she was listening until suddenly she'd say what was on her mind." Richard Salzman, another classmate who later became a judge in the Washington, D.C., Superior Court, insists Ruth was "never stuck up."

As she had done in elementary school, Ruth joined many groups and participated in many activities. She played the cello in the school orchestra, practiced piano, and became an accomplished baton twirler. She served as treasurer of the Go-Getters' Club, a student pep group for sports teams, and she helped to produce the high school yearbook. She also belonged to Arista, an honor society, and was a features editor of the school newspaper. She served as secretary to the English Department chairman, and even ran for office in student government.

Ruth spent her summers at Camp Che-Na-Wah, a girls' camp owned by her aunt and uncle, Cornelia and Saul Amster. Located in the Adirondack Mountains of northern New York, the Jewish camp was named for an Indian princess, and it combined Sabbath services and Native American rituals with athletics, arts and crafts, and dramatics. Each year, a camp bazaar raised funds that were donated to various charities.

Ruth was an all-around camper who especially enjoyed horseback riding. Friends remember that she was athletic and poised, although a bit shy. When Ruth was old enough, she became a counselor at Camp Che-Na-Wah. The swimming instructor, Ruth Wortman, recollects that young Ruth was a natural leader who served as "camper rabbi."

Many years later, a group of Che-Na-Wah campers sent Supreme Court justice Ginsburg letters of congratulations on her appointment. Ruth responded with words that echoed campfire ceremonies: "May the lamps of beauty, truth, fortitude, and love ever burn for the daughters of Camp Che-Na-Wah." A few years ago, Justice Ginsburg asked if she could bring her grandchildren to see the camp "while I can still paddle my own canoe," as she put it. Indeed, the agile grandmother was able to handle the craft and paddle at quite a clip.

Ruth's years at James Madison High School were a time of study, activities, and fun. They were also, however, a time of terrible tragedy for Ruth and her family. Just as Ruth was entering high school, her mother was diagnosed with cervical cancer. Ruth, whose biblical name recalls the loyalty and devotion of one woman to another, would sit by her mother's bedside and study while Celia rested.

Ruth did not tell her high school friends about her

During her years at James Madison High School, Ruth maintained her studies and activities while caring for her terminally ill mother. Graduating sixth in her class, she received several awards and honors.

mother's illness. Nor did she mention that the family business had begun to falter because Celia was increasingly unable to help Nathan manage the small furrier shop. When Celia died at home four years later, at age 47, she was surrounded by her loving family. In the years that followed people often commented about Ruth's stern demeanor; her own daughter kept a log of her mother's rare, cherished smiles. Beset with adult fears and concerns at an early age, Ruth did not enjoy a carefree adolescence. She came to realize during her impressionable years that life is precarious and precious.

Celia died just one day before Ruth's graduation from high school. Instead of attending her own graduation ceremonies, Ruth grieved at her mother's funeral. The many awards she had earned—including an English Scholarship Medal and the Parents' Association Award for Citizenship—were given to her later. Among her other honors were admission to the Round Table Forum of Honor and an honorable mention award for graduating sixth in her class out of more than 700 students. Ruth has spoken of her mother's "tremendous intellect" and respect for knowledge that inspired her to set lofty goals and strive to achieve them.

Years later, not long after Justice Ginsburg was appointed to the Supreme Court, her high school dedicated a mock courtroom to her. Ginsburg returned for the ceremony and joked that the room named in her honor was nicer than some of the real courtrooms in which she had practiced.

Still struggling with grief over her mother's death, Ruth left in the fall of 1950 for Cornell University in Ithaca, New York. Because of her top grades in high school, Ruth received a New York State scholarship as well as financial assistance from Cornell. She did, however, use most of the money her mother had saved for room and board. Alpha Epsilon Phi, one of the two Jewish sororities on campus, accepted Ruth as a member. She also belonged to the Women's Self-Governance Association.

Ruth's college years were a time when extreme gender discrimination favored male students over female students. Women were expected to marry and raise families rather than forge careers of their own. Female students were often taken less seriously in classes, since it was presumed that they would not work outside the home after they graduated. Ginsburg has said of those days at Cornell: "There was a problem with Cornell in the '50s. . . . The most important degree for you to get was Mrs., and it didn't do to be seen reading and studying." She added, "I knew some pretty obscure libraries on the Cornell campus."

Although Ruth certainly enjoyed dances, parties, and sporting events with her sorority sisters, she was determined to overcome the bias against female students. She applied herself to her studies with the same diligence she had exhibited in high school. Ruth's teachers included famed author and Russian émigré Vladimir Nabokov and Professor Robert E. Cushman, who taught constitutional law.

Nabokov was an inspiring teacher of literature who helped Ruth become a better reader and writer. Emphasizing style, character, and above all, language, Nabokov taught that even a single word can alienate or endear. Cushman, who later became Ruth's mentor, not only taught Ruth about government and constitutional law but also helped her hone the writing skills that would serve her well in her profession. He considered a clear, succinct prose style essential for all attorneys. From these gifted teachers Ruth learned that using words in a precise, convincing fashion is as necessary as it is rare.

In later years, Ruth wrote of this extremely formative period in her life:

> At Cornell, where I was an undergraduate, I was influenced particularly by . . . Professor Robert Cushman. I studied with him and worked as his research assistant. That was in the mid-1950s, an interesting time, the heyday of McCarthyism. Cushman was a defender of our deep-seated national values—freedom of thought, speech and press. He wasn't outspoken about it. He was a very gentle man. His own credentials were impeccable. But he could not tolerate threats to our American way, whether from the left or from the right. . . . That a lawyer could do something that was personally satisfying

During the Army-McCarthy hearings, Senator McCarthy himself was called as a witness to answer questions about his investigation. Here, he takes the oath to tell the truth on May 5, 1954.

The "Witch Hunts" of the 1950s

The early 1950s marked the beginning of the "cold war" between the Soviet Union and the United States. Many Americans feared that Communism would spread from the Soviet Union and Europe to the United States. Taking advantage of these fears, a relatively unknown Republican senator from Wisconsin, Joseph McCarthy, grabbed the spotlight when he claimed to have a list of more than 200 Communists who were working in the State Department.

Although no such list existed, McCarthy continued his attacks on people in the State Department, ruining several careers. Through his subcommittee, Investigations of the Senate Committee on Government Operations, McCarthy embarked on a campaign of reckless charges against alleged Communists in the government. Through smears and innuendos, he attacked high-ranking State Department officials and then expanded his investigations to include charges of espionage in the U.S. Army.

The Army-McCarthy hearings were the first televised U.S. congressional hearings, and as millions of Americans viewed them, they came to recognize the destructiveness of McCarthy's "witch hunt." The senator never found any Communists, and in December 1954 he was formally censured by the Senate for conduct "contrary to Senate traditions." McCarthy dropped from public view and died in 1957, but he left the nation with the term "McCarthyism," which is used to describe the threat to Americans' basic freedoms when people are falsely accused or are denied their constitutional rights.

and at the same time work to preserve the values that have made this country great was an exciting prospect for me.

Ruth's freshman year at Cornell was a momentous one for her personally. She met her future husband, Martin David Ginsburg, when they were introduced through a blind date. A sophomore from Long Island, Martin was an intercollegiate golfer and one of the few students to have a car on campus. When recalling his initial impressions of Ruth, Martin has said, "Ruth is a very quiet person. Our first date was a pleasant but undistinguished evening."

The two continued to date casually. Ruth has admitted that Martin was not a conscientious student but was a prolific reader. Although he may have failed remedial German and given up premedical training for golf, Ruth notes that her future husband was quite competitive in college. The two often took the same courses, and Martin tried to score higher than Ruth. "Once or twice he succeeded," Ruth quips. She also commented that Martin "was the only boy I knew who cared that I had a brain."

Martin himself recalls the attitudes toward women that existed during those years at Cornell. "Only about one in five students admitted were women, so of course the women tended to be smarter. Still, in the main these women had little interest in doing things. I never understood why that ought to be." Such progressive views about the role of women would surely be appealing to a young woman like Ruth.

And indeed they were. By 1953, friendship had flowered into romance, and the young couple became engaged. Ruth's cousin Jane Amster Gervitz recalls that she thought Martin was the "nicest" of all the boys Ruth knew, and she wondered when Ruth would realize that "Martin was her soulmate." When that day arrived, Ruth told Jane that she "never thought love could be like this."

Martin Ginsburg poses for a photo at the time of his engagement to Ruth. The couple celebrated their engagement at a party in New York City's Plaza Hotel.

Martin jokes that he and Ruth illustrate the theory that opposites attract. "We are not tremendously similar. I got the lowest passing grades in my class while she was the valedictorian of hers. I'm more talkative, but Ruth only speaks when she has something to say. That has never inhibited me. I like commercial subjects, and my wife has the 'disadvantage' of doing well at everything." He might also have

Ruth was in her third year at Cornell when she became engaged to Martin Ginsburg. As was customary at the time, Ruth posed for an "engagement" photo, too.

noted that they are "opposites" in height as well: Ruth is 5' 2" and Martin is 5' 11".

Martin graduated a year ahead of Ruth at Cornell, and he began his first year at Harvard University Law School in 1953. Although Ruth would not complete her undergraduate work for another year, she had applied to Harvard one year early—as was customary—and also been accepted. Both of them had decided to enter the same field of study—law.

Ruth graduated in 1954 from Cornell's College of Arts and Sciences with a bachelor of arts degree, high honors in government, distinction in all subjects, and membership in Phi Beta Kappa and Phi Kappa Phi honor societies. Just days after graduation, Ruth and Martin married. The small wedding, with 16 relatives in attendance, was held at the Ginsburg family home in Rockville Center, New York, on June 23.

Martin's father, Morris Ginsburg, had not completed high school, but he was a successful businessman. Martin's mother, Evelyn, had more education than her husband, but she stayed at home after they married to take care of the family and raise the children—as did most women of her generation. Mrs. Ginsburg became a wonderful mother-in-law to Ruth, while Mr. Ginsburg was like a second father to her.

Ruth's father, Nathan Bader, was nervous about his daughter's choice of law as a profession. He preferred that Ruth become a teacher because he had little money to leave Ruth, and he feared she would be unable to find a job in law. However, Ruth's father-in-law backed the young bride in whatever path she chose, even later, when Ruth became pregnant. As she recollected, "Early on my father-in-law said to me that . . . if I really wanted to be a lawyer, having a baby wouldn't stand in my way. I realized he was absolutely right, and I think he gave me sound advice for most things in life. If you want to do something badly enough, you find a way. Somehow you manage." Ruth also praised her mother-in-law's support. During Ginsburg's Rose Garden acceptance speech at the White House in 1993, the new Supreme Court nominee spoke of Evelyn Ginsburg as "the most supportive parent a person could have."

Because Martin had been drafted into the army during the Korean War, the newlyweds had to interrupt their education at Harvard Law School. However, they were fortunate when Martin received a deferral. For two-and-a-half months, Ruth and Martin traveled throughout Europe on a long honeymoon, visiting England, France, Italy, and Switzerland. Upon their return, they settled at Fort Sill, Oklahoma, where Lieutenant Martin Ginsburg was posted as an artillery officer.

Ruth's studies as a law student at both Harvard and Columbia University never prevented her from sharing the joys of family life with her daughter, Jane.

3

PREPARING FOR A CAREER

Ruth and Martin decided from the outset that they would share household chores. That included cooking meals, a skill at which Ruth did not excel. The new husband said of his wife's first cooked meal—a tuna casserole—that the dish was "as close to inedible as food could be." Martin began studying cookbooks. The couple also decided that however busy their lives might become, they would always try to share dinner together as a family—a pledge the Ginsburgs have generally been able to keep over the years.

Although Ruth had been accepted at Harvard Law School, she had to postpone her admission and thereby lost the scholarship she had received. While Martin fulfilled his military service, Ruth worked for the Lawton, Oklahoma, Social Security office. Her job made little use of her education in government or her appreciable intellectual abilities. Still, Ruth wanted to help others wherever she could. At her job, she saw that elderly Native Americans who did not have birth certificates were being denied Social Security benefits. Ruth awarded them benefits anyway, based on dates

Ruth and Martin as newly-weds share smiles at Fort Sill, Oklahoma, where Martin was stationed during the first two years of their marriage.

given on drivers' licenses or fishing licenses.

At Lawton, Ruth experienced her first unpleasant taste of discrimination in the workplace. When she innocently shared with supervisors the happy news of her pregnancy, she was demoted to a lower level with a reduced salary. Also, because she was pregnant, she was not allowed to travel across the country to Baltimore, Maryland, to attend a training session.

On July 21, 1955, Jane Carol Ginsburg was born, but not at Fort Sill. Instead, Martin took a leave from military duty so the couple could return to Long

Island, preferring the "local" hospital in Freeport, New York, to the army post hospital. Ruth stayed at home in Fort Sill the first year after Jane's birth to take care of her daughter. This was the only time in her marriage that Ruth did not work outside the home.

While caring for the baby, Ruth applied to Harvard Law School for a second time. She chose to study law for a number of reasons, including her strong writing abilities. She thought that journalism might require even more talent as a writer, and law would be "easier." The future Supreme Court justice also concluded that she had little artistic ability and so rejected the creative fields. Although Ruth felt secure about her reasoning and problem-solving skills, which are critical for lawyers, she still was wary of entering a field in which employment prospects for women were rather poor. However, she received unconditional encouragement and support from Martin and his family.

In 1956, with Martin's service completed, the three Ginsburgs moved to Cambridge, Massachusetts. Martin resumed his second year of law school at Harvard while Ruth began her first. She was only one of nine women in a class of more than 500 students.

Ruth and her female classmates did not receive an enthusiastic reception at Harvard. When Dean Erwin Griswold invited the female students to his home for dinner, he asked them to justify taking up places at the university that men could otherwise occupy. He and some of the other Harvard faculty had a basic distrust of women's abilities and questioned whether women should even have a right to enter the legal profession. Ruth modestly responded with answers that would not offend a law school dean whose question betrayed his position. She simply suggested that her purpose was to better understand her husband's work and possibly find a part-time job.

Years later, Ginsburg spoke of other instances of obvious discrimination. "When I attended the Harvard

Law School, there was no space in the dormitories for women. Women were not admitted to the Harvard Faculty Club dining tables. One could invite one's father but not one's wife or mother to the [*Harvard*] *Law Review* banquet."

Despite such obstacles, Ruth excelled at Harvard. Unlike many students who grumbled about the workload, Ruth enjoyed the challenge and appreciated master teachers who prompted students to think. "I loved the engagement with the materials—the lectures were absorbing," she said. She praised, for example, Benjamin Kaplan, who taught civil procedure, which subsequently became Ruth's principal field. Martin commented later that concentrating on procedure "teaches you to play the game straight."

Not only did Martin support Ruth's efforts at Harvard, but he also contributed a great deal to her success through his willingness to share parenting and household duties. After little Jane's babysitter left at 4:00 P.M. each day, Ruth and Martin took turns caring for their daughter and alternating evening chores so that the other one could study at the library. Justice Ginsburg has said about Martin and this time in her life:

> My husband is my biggest supporter. That was certainly true my first year in law school. Like all first-year law students, I had concerns about how I was doing in relation to all those brilliant people. My husband told his classmates and mine: "My wife is going to be on the *Law Review*."

Martin proved to be correct in his prediction. In 1957, Ruth was elected to the highly coveted editorship of the *Harvard Law Review*, a student journal covering legal issues. Even though her duties increased her workload, getting that position on the prestigious journal was a triumph for any woman.

A few months after Ruth's election to the *Law*

Review, Martin, in his third year of law school, was diagnosed with a life-threatening cancer that had spread to his lymph nodes. The prognosis was poor. According to Ruth's cousin Jane Gervitz, the illness "was like a sword hanging over their heads." As Martin underwent surgery and weeks of radiation treatment, the couple tried to be optimistic. They were determined to beat the disease.

Ruth remembers those days as the hardest in her

Cambridge, Massachusetts, became home to the Ginsburg family when Ruth entered the Harvard Law School in 1956. As one of only nine female students in a class of more than 500, Ruth encountered some of the same discrimination she had experienced at Cornell.

life. Although Martin had been able to attend classes at the end of the spring semester, because of the radiation therapy he felt well enough to study for only two hours a day, between midnight and 2:00 A.M. Harvard refused to accept any change in academic requirements or grading so that Martin could complete his studies over a longer period of time. Undaunted, Ruth arranged for various people to attend each of Martin's classes and take notes, which she used to help Martin study during the brief periods when he could concentrate.

From the beginning, Martin had loved tax law. While he was ill, the subject diverted his mind and provided some much-needed relief from a grueling medical ordeal. Fellow students brought notes to Martin's bedside, and Ruth remembers that "we wrote his senior paper together" during those early morning hours when Martin felt well. At the same time, Ruth maintained the high quality of her own studies, managed her home, and cared for a three-year-old child. With excellent tutors and "not too much cluttering his mind," Ruth noted, Martin caught up with his class and graduated with his classmates in 1958.

After graduation from Harvard, a recovered Martin Ginsburg landed a job with the New York City law firm of Weil, Gotshal, and Manges. Following her husband, Ruth transferred to the Columbia University Law School, also in New York City, where she was one of only 12 female students. Although Columbia was much like Harvard in its attitude toward female students, Ruth did find some open-minded professors who were impressed with her abilities.

Fellow student Richard Salzman remembers a class he and Ruth took with Professor Herbert Wechsler, who taught constitutional law. Professor Wechsler wrote an important casebook, documenting and commenting on many of the significant cases involving constitutional issues. Ruth would later use Wechsler's book in her own teaching and research. Salzman described a typical class: "There was a long table, and people chose seats as far away from him [Wechsler] as they could. We would wait five minutes because Ruth was always late; she had to run from another class that met far away." The second that Ruth arrived, Wechsler would ask a lengthy complicated question and call on Ruth. Not caught off guard, Ruth would explain in equal detail the information that was lacking to allow an adequate response. "I guess you're right, Mrs. Ginsburg," the professor conceded one day. "That question is far beyond the scope of this course."

Ruth attacked her studies with an energy that earned her the nickname "Ruthless Ruthie." In proving her worth, she earned the editorship of Columbia's *Law Review* and tied for first in her class. In 1959, Ruth graduated from Columbia with an LL.B. (Bachelor of Laws) degree and was admitted that same year to the New York bar. At Columbia's graduation ceremony, hundreds of people in the audience heard four-year-old Jane proudly proclaim: "That's my mommy!"

Ruth was ready to begin her career as a lawyer, or so she thought. Wearing a neatly tailored black "interview" suit bought by her mother-in-law, the star graduate began her search for a job. Ruth applied unsuccessfully to numerous private firms. She also applied for every clerkship in the U.S. district court for the southeast district. Even the law office in which Ruth had worked and excelled during summers did not hire her. Despite incredible credentials, "not a single law firm in the entire city of New York bid for my employment," she recalls.

The following year Supreme Court justice Felix Frankfurter refused to consider Ginsburg for a clerkship on the high court, even though she had been recommended by the professor at Harvard Law School who usually selected the justice's law clerks. Frankfurter had hired the first black clerk in 1948, but he was not ready to hire a woman. "Does she wear skirts?" he asked. "I can't stand girls in pants."

Chief Justice William Rehnquist and Justice Sandra Day O'Connor, the first woman on the U.S. Supreme Court, at a mock trial at the Stanford University Law School. Each justice had graduated from Stanford in 1952 at the top of the class, but each traveled a very different road to the Supreme Court.

It might appear that Ruth had some peculiar trait that alienated law firms that might otherwise have wanted to hire her. But that wasn't true. Consider the parallel experience of Sandra Day O'Connor, the very first woman to be appointed to the Supreme Court. Justice O'Connor graduated with top honors from Stanford Law School in 1952, as did Chief Justice William Rehnquist. After graduation, Rehnquist was offered a Supreme Court clerkship, but the high court refused to consider O'Connor, and no law office in the private sector would hire her either. "I interviewed with law firms in Los Angeles and San Francisco,"

Justice O'Connor recalls, "but none had ever hired a woman before as a lawyer, and they were not prepared to do so."

Being a woman may have been only one of the grounds upon which Ruth Bader Ginsburg faced prejudice. She recalls:

> In the '50s, the traditional law firms were just beginning to turn around on hiring Jews. In the '40s it was very difficult for a Jew to be hired in one of the well-established law firms. They had just gotten over that form of discrimination. But to be a woman, a Jew and a mother to boot, that combination was a bit much. Probably motherhood was the major impediment. The fear was that I would not be able to devote my full mind and time to a law job.

Of course, Ruth had been a woman, a Jew, and a mother throughout law school, none of which had interfered with the outstanding quality of her achievements. Ruth Bader Ginsburg was not a woman to surrender to bias, however. She persisted in her job search and finally found someone who was willing to give her a chance. She landed a position with Judge Edmund L. Palmieri as a law clerk at the U.S. District Court for the Southern District of New York. Her career in law had begun.

When Ruth embarked on her career as a professor of law, she found herself juggling work and family as well as her research and writing, just as she had done during her law school years.

4

PROFESSOR OF LAW

For two years Ruth Bader Ginsburg worked tirelessly to prove that Judge Palmieri had made the right choice in hiring her. "I worked harder than any other law clerk in the building, stayed late whenever it was necessary, sometimes when it wasn't necessary, came in Saturdays, and brought work home," said Ginsburg. The judge respected her dedication, and they soon became good friends. In future years, Ginsburg learned that one of her teachers had spent quite some time convincing Palmieri that she would make a fine law clerk and would not be running home constantly to care for her young child. Twenty years later, Judge Palmieri rated Ruth Bader Ginsburg as one of the best clerks he had ever had.

Throughout Ginsburg's clerkship, her legal research and writing were more than exemplary. When she completed her work with Judge Palmieri, his recommendations opened the way for future employment for her. Although she was offered positions in several law firms, she declined and instead accepted a two-year contract from Columbia University's International Procedure Project.

Justice Ginsburg explains why: "I did that for a few reasons, some clear to me then, others probably locked in my subconscious. One reason was the opportunity to write a book." She adds that since the book would deal with the Swedish judicial system, "Another attractive feature was going off to a foreign land I knew nothing about and being wholly on my own."

For several months before going abroad in 1962, Ginsburg was tutored in Swedish. Then, leaving Martin in New York City, she finally departed for the city of Lund and was soon joined by daughter Jane. The child, who had finished first grade, attended a day-care center while her mother worked. Ginsburg recalls that "the University of Lund, where I did much of my work, had a fine day-care center for children of students and faculty, just an excellent place. That kind of all-day center was just about unknown in the United States then."

The following year, Ginsburg spent two months in Stockholm, still accompanied by Jane. The little girl spent the summer at a rural camp located a few hours by train from Stockholm. Jane has recalled that she enjoyed the experience—except for the goat's milk, which she did not like.

Having completed her research, Ginsburg returned home in 1963 to finish the book *Civil Procedure in Sweden,* which she coauthored with Anders Bruzelius. The book was published two years later by M. Nijhoff, a Dutch publisher, in conjunction with Columbia University's Parker School of Foreign and Comparative Law. Jane, who was less than 10 years old at the time, helped "proofread" the manuscript.

With this research and writing completed, Ruth Bader Ginsburg had to consider her next career move. In 1963 Rutgers University in New Jersey was looking for an African-American man to replace one of its black law professors who had resigned. When the university could not locate an appropriate black faculty member who taught civil procedure, Rutgers did what it considered

"the next best thing" by searching for a woman to replace him. Ginsburg was offered the post, and she accepted it.

"I never thought it would be possible for me to be a law professor," she recollected years later. "There were only half a dozen women law professors across the country. I didn't want to teach that early. I wanted to be an advocate for four years or so, but such an opportunity wouldn't come again. I took what I could get."

Ginsburg considers the fact that she became one of the first women professors of law in the United States as a sign of *mazel*, or good luck, despite the personal tragedies that she experienced in her earlier years. This reflects the positive attitude that Justice Ginsburg has consistently maintained. "I consider myself a fantastically lucky person. So much in my childhood was not happy." Referring to her sister and mother, she says, "The smell of death was strong in my life," but she adds that "in love, I was lucky."

Law professor Ruth Bader Ginsburg (shown at far right) was always available to her students. She encouraged and supported them and became a role model, especially for the young women in her classes.

*In addition to her writings
and activities with many
law associations during her
teaching years, Ruth Bader
Ginsburg often attended
various conferences and
lectured at home and
abroad.*

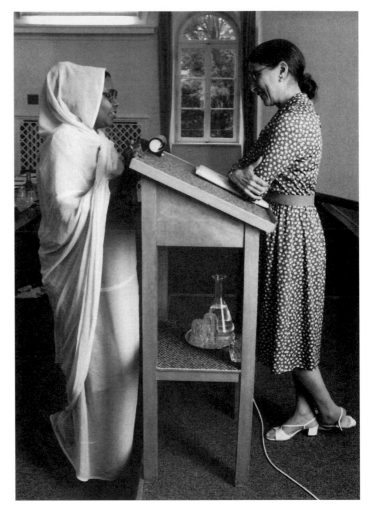

As an assistant professor at Rutgers School of Law, Ginsburg was the second woman ever to teach there. Although that very year Congress had passed the Equal Pay Act, making it illegal to pay men more than women for performing the same job, she still did not receive as much money as male faculty members of equal rank. She recalls the rationalization given for this discrimination: "The good dean of the law school carefully explained about the state university's limited resources and then added it was only fair to pay me modestly because my husband had a very good job." Seven years later, Ginsburg and other female faculty members filed a claim against the university to enforce the law. Each received a substantial increase in salary.

At the beginning of 1965, the Ginsburgs experienced another stroke of luck. Ten years after the couple was told they would not have any more children, Ruth became pregnant. Remembering her previous experience at Fort Sill, she disguised her pregnancy with baggy clothes and kept it secret. As an untenured professor on one-year contracts, she might have endangered her academic position if she had revealed her pregnancy. When the Ginsburgs welcomed James Steven into the world on September 8, 1965, Ruth Bader Ginsburg had already renewed her contract.

That same year, Ruth's father moved in with the family for several months to convalesce from severe injuries sustained in an auto accident. Despite the added responsibilities of caring for an infant and an elderly parent, Ruth continued to excel at her teaching and was soon promoted to associate professor.

Ginsburg taught at Rutgers until 1971. Following a brief teaching stint at Harvard Law School, she accepted a post at Columbia University's Law School in 1972. She became the school's first full-time female professor and the first female faculty member to receive lifetime tenure. From 1972 until 1980, Professor Ginsburg gave courses in constitutional law and civil procedure. One of Ginsburg's students, Deborah Jones Merritt, has praised her professor's teaching: "In three years of law school, Ruth Bader Ginsburg was my only female professor—but what a professor! Ginsburg was a precise and thoughtful teacher, a nationally admired advocate, and an extraordinary role model."

Ginsburg thoroughly enjoyed teaching. She has explained it this way: "I liked the sense of being my own boss. . . . There's a tremendous luxury in being a law teacher in that you can spend most of your time doing whatever interests you."

About her own teaching style, Ginsburg said:

> I don't pretend to be neutral on issues when I am not. I like the students to understand that most of us have a perspective, most thinking people do, but that it's important to disclose one's biases. I'm not trying to brainwash people, but I'm not going to present myself as neutral. I don't think my students have any doubt where I stand on the Bill of Rights.

The very first month that Ginsburg was at Columbia, she became involved in a discrimination incident. For economic reasons, the university laid off several cleaning women while retaining all the male janitors whose jobs were similar to those of the cleaning ladies. Ginsburg remembers, "I entered that fray, which happily ended with no layoffs, and, as I recall, the union's first female shop steward."

Ruth and Martin had hectic working schedules, but they were determined not to neglect their family life. As they had decided early in their marriage, the couple continued to share domestic responsibilities. While Martin was well on his way to becoming one of the top tax lawyers in America, he did much of his work at home so that he could help take care of the children. During that time he tried out recipes from various cookbooks and became a self-taught gourmet chef. In the beginning, he did not cook during the week but mainly on Sundays and for company. Jane remembers that her mother, on the other hand, "cooked badly," regularly inflicting on the family such culinary disasters as burnt pot roast.

The Ginsburgs were relatively strict parents. Martin was more likely to carry out punishments, such as taking away television privileges, while Ruth maintained a stony silence. "When I did something bad . . . my mother would be real quiet," Jane has reported. "While Dad was more vocal and demonstrative, Mom was aggressively disappointed."

The fact that her mother worked outside the home seemed normal to Jane, who attended Brearley, a private

Ruth strolls on the Harvard campus with daughter Jane (right). Following in her mother's footsteps, Jane also attended Harvard, became a lawyer, and went on to be a law professor at Columbia University. They were the first mother and daughter to serve on the same law faculty in the United States.

girls' school in New York City. Neighbors and some classmates, however, found her mother's professorship strange. It was for some, said Jane, "like a communicable disease." James, too, thought that a mother having a career was nothing unusual, but he was perplexed when people always "asked what my father did for a living. I wondered why they didn't ask what my mom did, which was more interesting."

What Mom did, in addition to her teaching, was spend hours poring over the many legal cases she was involved in at the time. James remembers that when living in New York City, he would awake in the middle of the night and find his mother in the dining room

Family vacations were a special time for Martin and Ruth, shown here with son James (center) and daughter Jane (right) in the Caribbean. James especially liked to vacation there as he and his mother could ride horses along island beaches.

"scribbling on drafts, with a cup of stale coffee and a box of prunes" amid "neat piles of paper that covered the entire table. Mom would work until the wee hours of the morning."

Despite her heavy schedule, Ruth Bader Ginsburg was deeply involved in her children's lives. Working from home, she could cast her watchful eye on them, keeping close track of their activities and supervising their homework. When much later, Jane introduced her mother at a public event, the daughter recalled, "Far from lacking maternal attention, I often felt I received entirely too much of it. My mother always seemed to know what I was doing, down to small details—such as 'You ate a candy bar yesterday.'" James, too, later joked that his mother was "always there when I wanted her to be—and even when I didn't." He added, however, that

"I became a much better writer because Mom always made me rewrite many drafts of my papers."

Ginsburg also found time to enjoy her favorite activities. She read, attended the opera, played golf, listened to classical music, saw old movies, and indulged in horseback riding and boating. She is a fine equestrian and, as her son has noted, plays golf "in the same deliberative fashion" with which she attacks everything in life. She takes her time. Others have also commented on Ginsburg's unique style. During a 50th-birthday tribute to her, one guest likened her golf swing to her politics: "She stands left, swings right, and hits straight down the middle."

Ruth and Martin not only cared about their children's physical and intellectual growth, but they also helped to develop their cultural life. Ruth spent many weekends with Jane at Broadway shows and performances of children's theater in New York City. James especially enjoyed attending the young people's concerts of the New York Philharmonic with his father. And the whole family went to operas at the Metropolitan Opera House and New York State Theater as often as possible. The parents also taught their children respect for the values, traditions, and customs of different cultures and societies. For instance, James, although raised in the Jewish faith, was encouraged to attend Sunday church services with one of the family's housekeepers, a devout Christian, to be introduced to other religions.

Many years later, Ginsburg wrote an article in which she quoted a University of Michigan survey that found that of all its law school graduates, women lawyers with children and family obligations were the most content. Ruth included this research in her article because it expressed an essential truth of her life.

Throughout her career, Ruth Bader Ginsburg has been a staunch and untiring supporter of women's rights. She argued numerous cases before the courts, advocating equal protection for women under the law.

5

AN ADVOCATE FOR WOMEN'S RIGHTS

n the early 1960s, Ruth Bader Ginsburg read a book called *The Second Sex*, a landmark feminist work by the French writer Simone de Beauvoir. The more Ginsburg read, the more she began to recognize that the second-class treatment she had experienced in the workplace was a symptom of a broader social bias that denied women choices and opportunities open to men. The law, she came to believe, should be a tool for redressing these inequities.

As a well-known law professor, writer, and member of several law associations, Ginsburg received sex-discrimination cases referred to her by the American Civil Liberties Union (ACLU). The organization is dedicated to protecting the civil rights of all Americans. As Ginsburg read the legal literature on the subject, she became more and more convinced that the law discriminated against women in nearly all areas of their lives. As she later indicated, "Once I became involved [in sex-discrimination cases], I found the legal work fascinating and had high hopes for significant change in the next decade."

Ginsburg did get an opportunity to cause a significant change to take place. In 1971 the ACLU asked her to be the principal author of a brief (a legal argument supporting or opposing a particular position) to present to the Supreme Court. The brief involved the case of *Reed v. Reed*. Sally Reed, a woman from Idaho, sought to overturn a state law that gave preference to a man (her former husband) over a woman (herself) in administering the estates of deceased relatives. In this case, the deceased relative was the Reeds' son, who had committed suicide after his father took custody away from the mother.

The basis for the Idaho law was the assumption that a man is more capable than a woman in administering estates. It was up to the woman to prove she was capable. Ginsburg's brief argued that in this case, it was up to the state to prove that the man was more capable than the woman. Ginsburg and the ACLU won a major victory when the Supreme Court struck down the Idaho law. As she noted, "It was the first time the Supreme Court ever overturned a law in response to a woman's complaint of unfair sex-based discrimination." Ginsburg's arguments became known as the "grandmother brief" because it was the ancestor of many future opinions on women's rights.

Responding to this victory, the ACLU set up the Women's Rights Project to handle cases of "sex stereotyping." Ginsburg was named codirector with Brenda Feigen Fasteau, who managed the organization's daily operations while Ginsburg handled litigation and research. "Our idea was to try to find the right cases, bring them before the most sympathetic tribunals, and help develop constitutional law in the gender classification area step by step," Ruth explained. At the time a tenured professor at Columbia Law School, Ginsburg arranged to devote half her time to the Women's Rights Project. She soon gained other positions at the ACLU. In 1973, Ruth Bader Ginsburg was appointed the

In the 1970s and 1980s, women across the nation rallied, demonstrated, and protested against inequality. These demonstrators are agitating for the passage of ERA, the proposed Equal Rights Amendment to the Constitution.

organization's general counsel. The following year, she became a member of the ACLU's national board of directors.

During her time with the Women's Rights Project, Ginsburg brought six cases dealing with sex discrimination before the Supreme Court—and won five of them. According to Kathleen Peratis, who worked for her as staff director, "It was a heady time. We won everything. We thought it would never end."

In arguing cases, Ginsburg took the strategy of challenging laws that appeared to benefit women but that actually reflected sex discrimination. By often suing on the behalf of men, she brought attention to the importance of *equal* protection for women under the law. During the 1970s Ginsburg avoided such controversial issues as abortion rights, concentrating on cases she believed she could win. As Kathleen Peratis described Ginsburg's strategy, she "had a real vision of where she wanted to go and what she had to do to get there." Ginsburg's colleague Brenda Fasteau also commented on Ginsburg, saying, "She saw the big picture."

Ginsburg got the opportunity to sue on behalf of a man in her second major argument before the Supreme Court. In this case she appeared in person before the Court for the first time. She took on unfair practices in the military in the 1973 case of *Frontiero v. Richardson.*

The plaintiffs (people filing the suit) were Air Force lieutenant Sharron Frontiero and her husband, Joseph. Richardson, the defendant, was Eliot L. Richardson, then secretary of defense, who had the overall responsibility for the military. The Frontieros objected to a statute under which a man in military service automatically gained benefits for his wife even if she did not depend on his income. It was generally assumed that a wife was dependent. However, in order for a husband to gain benefits from a wife in the service, the wife had to prove that she provided more than half of her husband's financial support.

Because of the statute, Joseph Frontiero had been denied his wife's benefits. The issue in the case was the fact that the families of men serving in the military could receive benefits, whereas the families of women, also serving in the military, could not. In effect, the case was one of equal pay for women.

Arguing before the nine Supreme Court justices was intimidating at first. Ginsburg was so nervous she feared she "couldn't keep down breakfast." Once she began speaking, however, she felt a surge of power. For the duration of the time allotted to her, the justices listened attentively.

At the close of her argument, Ginsburg quoted Sarah Grimke—the 19th-century feminist who wrote: "I ask no favor for my sex. All I ask of our brethren is that they take their feet off our necks. . . . Thank you." Her presentation was so impressive that eight of the nine justices voted in favor of the Frontieros. As a result of this case, the military changed the rules defining dependency, making them the same for men and women who serve in the military.

The one case Ginsburg lost while working for the Women's Rights Project involved a Florida law that permitted widows but not widowers to take a small deduction from their real property taxes. In *Kahn v. Shevin,* Ginsburg challenged a law that seemed to favor women. She believed, however, that the law hurt the status of women because it assumed they were inferior and needed more help than men.

Ginsburg was unable to persuade a majority of the justices in this case, and the Florida law remained unchanged. Later, she began to understand part of the reason. Justice William O. Douglas, possibly the most liberal member of the Supreme Court and one who normally supported women's rights, had voted in favor of the Florida law. In reading Douglas's autobiography, Ginsburg discovered that Douglas's mother had been a struggling widow who had faced great hardship raising her son. Perhaps Justice Douglas was willing to give widows a little extra, recognizing the crushing difficulties many of them encountered.

Ginsburg was particularly interested in cases involving Social Security as she had worked in a Social Security office in Oklahoma many years earlier and had first-hand experience of discrimination there. In 1975, in *Weinberger v. Wiesenfeld,* Ginsburg argued in support of Stephen Wiesenfeld and his fight for Social Security benefits. Wiesenfeld's wife had died in childbirth, leaving him with an infant son to raise. Stephen wanted to stay home to care for the child. To meet expenses, he needed

The Road to Equality for Women

In 1848, Elizabeth Cady Stanton and Lucretia Mott organized the Women's Rights Convention and demanded equal rights for women under the law. They began a movement that has sometimes slowed but has never stopped. A major goal of the early women's movement was to obtain the right to vote. To fight for this right, Stanton and Susan B. Anthony founded the National Woman Suffrage Association in 1869. Fifty years later, women finally received the right to vote. Some further progress was made from the 1920s through the 1940s as a few women entered Congress, became state governors, and held government posts. It was not until the 1960s, however, that the first powerful women's group since the 19th century was formed to push for greater power and civil rights for women—the National Organization for Women. One of the organization's founders and its first president was Betty Friedan. Her landmark book, *The Feminine Mystique*, was instrumental in changing women's ideas about their personal, economic, and political status in American society. Women from all walks of life protested, demonstrated, and agitated for equal rights. As a result of these actions, in the following decades the Supreme Court heard many test cases in which it ruled that the gender discrimination found in a variety of laws and regulations was illegal.

the extra money from the survivor benefits that he thought his wife's employment had secured for him.

The Social Security Administration denied Wiesenfeld's claim and informed him that he would not receive benefit payments. Wiesenfeld sued the Social Security Administration, and his case eventually reached the Supreme Court. At the time, women could claim survivor benefits based on their husbands' employment, but men could not claim benefits based on their wives' employment. The law was founded on the assumption that husbands were always wage earners and wives were always dependent caregivers. In Wiesenfeld's case, the child and the father were both hurt by a discriminatory law. In attacking this form

Betty Friedan, one of the leaders of the women's movement, gives a speech at the 1995 International Women's Forum, held in the People's Republic of China.

of gender bias, Ginsburg contended that the law "must deal with the parent, not the mother; with the home-maker, not the housewife; and with the surviving spouse, not the widow." The judges struck down the law. However, they did so more for the sake of the child than for the equal treatment of widows and widowers.

Ginsburg won another case in 1977 involving Social Security in *Califano v. Goldfarb*, which she once again argued before the Supreme Court. Goldfarb, an elderly man whose wage-earning wife had recently died, was denied survivor benefits that would automatically have been given to a woman. Not having been independently covered under Social Security, Goldfarb wanted to

In addition to her activities with scores of organizations, Ruth Bader Ginsburg has also received numerous honors. Here she speaks after receiving an honorary degree from De Paul University in Chicago.

collect survivor benefits from his wife's account. Ginsburg argued that a female worker should have the same protection for her family as a male worker. The justices agreed, and that provision of the Social Security Act was struck down.

Ginsburg also took on her first case dealing with the issue of women's service on juries. The case involved a Louisiana law that declared women exempt from jury duty unless they volunteered. And not many did at the time. Ginsburg stated that women involved in trials or lawsuits should have the right to a jury of their peers. Exempting women from jury duty meant that few female peers would ever contribute to this key aspect of American justice. Ginsburg's arguments were convincing, and the Louisiana law was invalidated.

Thanks to Ginsburg's arguments in 1978 in the case of *Duren v. Missouri*, the Supreme Court also struck down a Missouri law that relieved women of jury duty if they requested an exemption. She contended that the Missouri law showed that the state gave lesser value to women's citizenship than to men's. Following these two victories, the Supreme Court ruled that state jury-selection systems could not exempt women as a class.

In the following year Ginsburg filed a "friend of the court" brief in the Supreme Court, arguing that an Oklahoma law restricting the purchase of alcohol by young people discriminated against young men and was unconstitutional. The legal age for men to purchase low-alcohol beer was 21; women could legally buy it at 18. The basis for the law appeared to be that young men would be more likely to be drunk drivers than women. Although the law seemed to view young women as more responsible than young men, Ginsburg argued a different point. She noted that the "familiar stereotype: the active boy, aggressive and assertive; the passive girl, docile and submissive" should not be legalized. The Supreme Court overturned the Oklahoma law.

Among the other cases on which Ginsburg worked was one that successfully challenged a New Jersey state regulation requiring pregnant teachers to quit their jobs without any right to return to work following the birth of their babies. As in many of the other cases that attorney Ginsburg handled, she had the chance to help women who were exposed to the same types of discrimination she had encountered in her life.

During the 1970s, many of the cases supporting women's rights that Ginsburg argued dealt with the rights of pregnant women, who were often not allowed to return to their jobs after their children were born.

Ginsburg also addressed issues dealing with the use of sick leave for pregnancy and the loss of seniority for women following the birth of a baby.

Through the women's movement of the 1970s and 1980s and through the courts, women made great advancements in gaining equal rights. And Ruth Bader Ginsburg was instrumental in changing the legal landscape for women. Nevertheless, not everyone supported equal rights for women. Some critics argued that

Ginsburg's approach failed to take into account very real differences between men and women that might support preferential treatment for men. Ginsburg's view is that using the skills and talents of all Americans, rather than eliminating more than half the population from consideration, will ultimately raise standards for both men and women.

When asked about general differences between men and women, Ginsburg says:

> Generalizations about the way women or men are—my life experience bears out—cannot guide me reliably in making decisions about particular individuals. At least in the law, I have found no natural superiority or deficiency in either sex. In class or in grading papers from 1963 until 1980, and now in reading briefs and listening to arguments in court for over 17 years, I have detected no reliable indicator of distinctly male or surely female thinking or even penmanship.

Ginsburg's career moved steadily ahead when she was appointed to a federal judgeship on the U.S. Court of Appeals for the District of Columbia Circuit. She gained a reputation as a fair and open-minded judge who was committed to protecting the rights of all Americans.

6

ON THE BENCH

In 1980, President Jimmy Carter nominated Ruth Bader Ginsburg to a position on the U.S. Court of Appeals for the District of Columbia Circuit. This court is widely regarded as the second-highest court in the nation. With her superb background, Ginsburg was quickly approved and sworn into office on June 30. She was only the second female judge to sit on any of the nation's appeals courts.

An appeals (or appellate) court reviews judgments passed by other courts. Each state is assigned to one of 11 regional appellate-court circuits, or areas. The D.C. circuit, where Ginsburg would serve with 10 other federal judges, is different from the regional appellate circuits. Panels of three judges hear a large number of important cases in which the federal government is involved either as a plaintiff or defendant.

Generally, cases come to appellate courts from 89 district courts around the United States and, especially important in the D.C. circuit, from agencies of the federal government. Parties in lower courts who disagree with a judgment can appeal to a higher court, where judges read briefs from lawyers supporting or opposing the appeal. The panels of judges on the D.C. circuit hear the attorneys' arguments and decide whether to uphold or reverse lower-court decisions. Like the Supreme Court, the U.S. district courts and appeals courts are federal. They hear cases that may involve nationwide laws or constitutional issues.

For nearly 10 years Ginsburg had worked as an advocate. She had actively argued in favor of one position, representing the interests of her client and the interpretation of the law she passionately believed should be upheld. As a lawyer, Ginsburg argued for judges to interpret issues the way she did and solve problems in a similar manner. As a judge, however, she would have to be objective and listen more passively to both sides of an issue. Judicial temperament requires a person to put aside personal feelings and experiences while ruling fairly in each instance. Gerald Gunther, a professor and friend of Ginsburg, noted at her installation ceremony that a good judge is "open-minded and detached."

Ginsburg would later write her own evaluation of an effective judge as one who "strives to persuade and not to pontificate. She speaks in a moderate and restrained voice, engaging in a dialogue with, not a diatribe against, co-equal departments of government, state authorities, and even her own colleagues."

Ginsburg contrasted her role as an appeals judge to that of trial-court judges, whom she referred to negatively as "lords of their individual fiefdoms." Ginsburg explained that "no single court of appeals judge can carry the day in any case. To attract a second vote and establish durable law for the circuit, a judge may find it necessary to moderate her own position sometimes to be less bold, other times to be less clear." Ruth Bader Ginsburg saw her judicial role as one in which she would teach, learn, and convince through moderation rather than press her position in an adversarial manner.

Some observers thought President Jimmy Carter had appointed Ruth Bader Ginsburg to the appeals court in order to garner women's votes in the 1980 election. Whether this was true or not, his choice helped advance the cause of women as Justice Ginsburg continued to fight against bias in the law and the courts.

To accept her appointment as a federal judge, the Ginsburgs had to move to Washington, D.C. Martin gave up his New York law practice and his teaching post at Columbia University and became a professor of tax law at Georgetown University Law Center. He also joined the Washington office of the New York law firm of Fried, Frank, Harris, Shriver, and Jacobson. Martin jokes, "I've been trying to retire since 1978, but I'm not very good at it."

The Ginsburgs moved into the Watergate apartments in the nation's capital, where their ground-floor duplex overlooked the Potomac River. James was a

With Ruth Bader Ginsburg's appointment to the circuit court, the Ginsburgs moved to Washington, D.C.

teenager at the time, and he remembers the beautiful view of Rock Creek Park and the sunsets he could see from his bedroom window. An energetic lad, James enjoyed the pool and patio that were part of the complex and the miles of running trails in the park. Jane had already graduated from high school and begun college, but James feels that he "grew up in Washington."

During her 13 years on the appeals court, Ginsburg would gain a reputation as a strong, fair judge. A White House report described her as "tough on crime, committed to free speech and freedom of religion, and supportive of civil rights." Critics sometimes chided Judge Ginsburg for her friendship with one of the most conservative of her colleagues, Judge Antonin Scalia. However, she most often agreed with Judge Harry T. Edwards, who had been appointed by a Democratic president. Being friendly with a conservative did not affect her views. She heard every case on its merits and made up her mind without regard to politics or friendship.

On the bench, Judge Ginsburg's major opinions reflected her firmly held views on constitutional issues such as freedom of religion and speech. A 1984 case of religious freedom involved a Jewish air force officer whose commander denied him the right to wear his yarmulke (skullcap) while on duty. The majority of judges upheld the decision supporting the military. Judge Ginsburg voted to rehear the case and wrote a dissenting opinion. She declared that the military's refusal to let the officer wear his yarmulke expressed a "callous indifference" to his faith.

Judge Ginsburg also dissented from the majority when she supported a statute allowing attorneys to be appointed as independent counsels to represent the United States in investigating wrongdoing by high-level government officials. She firmly believed that no one in the United States was above the law. In 1988, the Supreme Court reversed the D.C. circuit's decision and upheld Judge Ginsburg's position on the constitutionality of the independent counsel statute. (This is the law that eventually allowed President Bill Clinton to be investigated during his last term in office.)

In 1989, Judge Ginsburg again dissented in a case involving federal funds and abortion. The Reagan administration had barred foreign family-planning organizations from receiving federal aid if the organization used funds from other, non-U.S. sources to inform women about abortions or to perform abortions. The majority of the court upheld the order. Judge Ginsburg, however, maintained that the government's actions violated the First Amendment right of domestic

As an appeals court judge, Ruth spent many hours working in her office, pictured here with files of her cases spread over the desk and shelves of legal reference books behind her. She reviewed each case meticulously, often working late into the night.

family-planning organizations to seek foreign partners to work with them.

Judge Ginsburg's clear thinking, careful reasoning, and assiduous preparation for every case won her the admiration of colleagues both liberal and conservative. She gained a reputation for asking lawyers penetrating questions that uncovered the central issues of each of their cases. She promptly drafted opinions assigned to her with scrupulous attention to detail. Years of litigation had taught her the impact such decisions would have on the lives of the people involved.

Sensitive to conditions outside the cloistered halls of justice, Judge Ginsburg often led law clerks on periodic tours of institutions housing less fortunate citizens. Deborah Jones Merritt, one of Judge Ginsburg's first law clerks at the D.C. circuit court, recalls her boss taking all three of her clerks to visit the D.C. jail, Lorton Penitentiary, and St. Elizabeth's Mental Hospital. With her law clerks, Judge Ginsburg had not only a professional relationship but also one of maternal kindness. She treated them to outings at the opera and hosted bridal showers, birthday parties, and other celebrations.

Another of Judge Ginsburg's law clerks, Peter Huber, in writing a tribute to her work, remembers that many of the cases they worked on in 1982 involved truck deregulation. The cases were very complex as well as incredibly boring. Nevertheless, Judge Ginsburg pored over these cases as thoroughly as she would a major constitutional issue.

Huber described an incident that occurred when working with her late at night on one of these cases. He recalls "a small lady framed by the bookshelves behind her, and a large desk, with [the files] open and spread about around her. . . . She smiled a truly contented smile, a smile of deep pleasure and satisfaction, and said—with *complete* sincerity—'Peter, I think I've finally worked it out. This is an absolutely *fascinating* case.'"

Huber went on to write: "Lots of judges will give you their best on the grand legal [issues], like the First Amendment or equal protection. But with Ruth Ginsburg, it's the law itself that's grand. The means, not the ends. You see it in every opinion she writes, large or small."

Judge Harry Edwards, a good friend and colleague of Judge Ginsburg, who is now chief judge of the D.C. circuit court, characterizes her as an extremely principled person who is "formidable" and "meticulous."

What Edwards describes as her "loyalty to family, friends, and colleagues" is reflected in an incident involving discrimination. A country club to which both the Ginsburg and the Edwards families had belonged suddenly changed its rules about who could be a member of the club. The new rules discriminated against African Americans, which made it impossible for people like the Edwardses to belong. Ruth and Martin promptly resigned from the establishment and insisted they would never return unless the Edwardses were permitted to join.

In keeping with her opposition to discrimination of any kind, Judge Ginsburg worked to improve the attitudes of the nation's courts toward women and minorities. She was part of a task force on gender, racial, and ethnic fairness in the courts, and she wrote the foreword to a report issued by the task force. Ginsburg explained that the federal courts should examine their actions and attitudes in order to improve their treatment of women and minorities and root out bias and unconscious prejudice. She urged the creation of educational programs so that judges, attorneys, and support personnel would become sensitive to unfair practices.

In her comments, Ginsburg cited, for example, a New York judge's opinion written in 1970 that upheld a law excusing women from jury duty. The judge had written that because of the "state of womanhood," which "prefers cleaning and cooking, rearing of children and television soap operas, bridge and canasta, the beauty parlor and shopping, to becoming embroiled in plaintiffs' problems," women did not have to serve on juries. Ginsburg observed that such a disrespectful description of women was frequently not even recognized as offensive. She stressed the need for reform in law school education so that judges would realize that deprecating any group of people has no place in courts of law.

The report of the task force found that 27 percent

of female judges had seen lawyers display bias toward female witnesses and litigants (those bringing lawsuits). The lawyers had ignored the women, interrupted them, or made disparaging comments. In recognizing that slights to women were sometimes unconscious, Ginsburg recounted her own experience. "Countless times during my 13 years' service on the D.C. circuit, when I attended a social event and was introduced to a stranger as Judge Ginsburg, the person would extend his hand to my husband—who invariably shook it."

The task force's report recommended that the circuit courts "address vital work-life concerns for court employees, in particular: family leave, flex-time, and child-care policies." Ginsburg concluded by pointing out that "the report indicates both how far we have

Until the 1970s, as in many of the top universities, male students far outnumbered female students in classes at Harvard. Ruth Bader Ginsburg deplored this bias, which she made every attempt to rectify through her decisions as a judge on the appellate court.

Although Martin was plagued by health problems, he and Ruth were cheered as they welcomed their first grandchild—Jane's son, Paul Bertrand, shown here with his grandparents in 1987.

come and the distance still before us as we work to achieve our aspirations of equality and fairness for the federal courts."

Ruth and Martin did not allow their busy professional lives to keep them from sharing a full and happy family life. In 1986, Ruth and Martin welcomed their first grandchild, Paul Bertrand Spera. Daughter Jane had married attorney George Spera Jr. in 1981. After graduating from college and working as a law clerk and then as a lawyer in a New York City firm, Jane had received a Fulbright Award to study abroad. The couple moved to France, where George joined the Paris office of a New York law firm.

The Spera's son, Paul, was born in Paris, and problems following the birth made Jane's recovery difficult. Ruth recalls talking to her daughter on the phone in an attempt to console her and cheer her up. "It was not a good time at all. She called me from the hospital, and we talked for two hours. I remember telling her that soon this baby will love you more than anyone in the world. And when we'd hung up, I thought, 'Gee, I must have done something right as a parent. When my daughter was feeling really low, she didn't call a friend. She called me. She called her mother.'"

Also in the late 1980s, Martin was beset by heart problems. In 1987, he underwent triple bypass heart surgery. The operation was a success, and Martin recovered, although afterwards he was plagued with recurring back problems. The couple could no longer share in their golf games. Still, they continued to travel together, teaching and lecturing throughout the world.

Capping a long and distinguished career, Ruth Bader Ginsburg takes the oath of office as the 107th justice to sit on the Supreme Court. Ruth's husband, Martin, holds the Bible. Chief Justice William Rehnquist, before whom she had appeared to argue the cause of women's rights, swears her in as President Bill Clinton looks on.

7

THE SUPREME COURT

The nine justices of the Supreme Court serve for life—or until they choose to retire—and are charged with interpreting our nation's laws in light of the Constitution. This makes nominating judges to the Supreme Court among the most important duties presidents perform. When President Bill Clinton was searching for a nominee to the Supreme Court to replace retiring justice Byron White, he said he was looking for someone with "a fine mind, good judgment, wide experience in the law and problems of real people, and someone with a big heart."

For three months the president and his advisers considered more than 40 candidates. In the final days before the choice was made, men were still the front-runners to join the "brethren," as Supreme Court justices are sometimes called. When Clinton turned his attention to Ginsburg, he decided to speak with her personally at the White House because he had met her only briefly many years before. On Sunday, June 13, 1993, the president and Judge Ruth Bader Ginsburg talked in a drawing room on the second floor of the White House for an hour and a half about Ginsburg's views and experience.

Clinton told the press that during this critical conversation, he realized that he had found the person he was seeking. Twelve hours after the meeting, the president phoned Ginsburg to inform her that she was his choice to be the 107th justice on the Supreme Court. The ceremony in the White House Rose Garden announcing Ginsburg's nomination was a triumph for her. Pending her confirmation by the U.S. Senate, she would have even more power to help protect the freedom of citizens throughout the nation.

In July 1993, millions of Americans watched on television as Ruth Bader Ginsburg appeared before the Judiciary Committee of the Senate, which would either confirm or deny her nomination. In her even-tempered, deliberative style of speech, Ginsburg expertly fielded the senators' questions on issues that included capital punishment, abortion, gay rights, discrimination, and the role of the courts. In her opening statement to the senators, she explained at the outset that her responses to specific questions would have to reflect "impartiality."

"Because I am and hope to continue to be a judge," Ginsburg explained, "it would be wrong for me to say or to preview in this legislative chamber how I would cast my vote on questions the Supreme Court may be called up to decide. Were I to rehearse here what I would say and how I would reason on such questions, I would act injudiciously."

On whether or not capital punishment is constitutional, for instance, she refused to forecast decisions she might be called upon to make as a justice. She even chided Senator Orrin Hatch, who pressed her on the question, that to preview such decisions was something "you must not ask a judge to do."

When Senator Edward Kennedy questioned her on discrimination, Ginsburg responded that she believed "rank discrimination" was un-American.

Rank discrimination, she explained, would occur "if I discriminated against some person for reasons that are irrelevant to that person's talent or ability." Pressed further on the sensitive issue of discrimination based on sexual orientation, she replied that she would give "no hints, no forecasts, no previews" on the question.

On abortion, however, Ginsburg did not use the "impartial" argument to stop her from expressing to the committee her wholehearted support of abortion rights. Before her nomination, Ginsburg had been criticized by some women's groups for statements she made about the Supreme Court's controversial decision in the *Roe v. Wade* case in 1973.

In *Roe v. Wade*, the Supreme Court had overturned state laws that made abortion illegal. The Court's ruling was based on the concept that a woman's right to privacy protects her decision about whether or not to bear a child. Ginsburg's view was that the ruling should have been based not on privacy but on the equal protection clause of the Fourteenth Amendment. She also felt that the decision was written in such a sweeping manner that it prevented a consensus throughout the nation and risked a backlash.

As part of the confirmation process, Ginsburg also had to disclose her family's financial dealings. President Clinton had experienced some problems with other federal nominees who had neglected to make Social Security payments for employees. It was essential for the Ginsburgs to prove they had abided by the law. There was no problem. In her own thorough way, Ginsburg had kept all employee records and had filed all employment returns. She had no trouble accounting for every penny paid to every employee.

Other financial documents released to the Judiciary Committee revealed that the Ginsburgs had a net worth of $6.1 million—making her the wealthiest member of the Supreme Court. For people of such wealth, however, the Ginsburgs lived quite modestly.

Ruth Bader Ginsburg appears on the first day of her Senate confirmation hearings. Republican and Democratic senators were impressed with her demeanor. Even the most conservative among them applauded her responses to their questions.

In 1993, they drove a six-year-old Nissan and an eight-year-old Volvo. They did not own a country home or other residences. Unlike many affluent people, the Ginsburgs did not make ostentatious purchases.

Confirmed by an overwhelming vote of 97 to 3, Ruth Bader Ginsburg took the oath of office as a Supreme Court justice on August 10, 1993. In the East

Room of the White House, Chief Justice William Rehnquist administered the oath of office as Martin and President Clinton stood by. There was some irony in taking the oath from Rehnquist. A junior justice on the Court when Ginsburg had argued a case as an attorney, Rehnquist had remarked, "So, Ms. Ginsburg, you won't settle for Susan B. Anthony's face on the new dollar, will you?" Ginsburg did not respond at the time, but the perfect response occurred to her later— "No, Justice Rehnquist. Tokens won't do."

Once Justice Ginsburg took her place on the bench, Court watchers and the media were not sure what to expect from the newest member of the Supreme Court. Some thought she could bring harmony to a divided body because of her reputation as a consensus builder. Yet, as a judge, she had cast many dissenting votes and had extolled the American judicial system for having the strength to embrace disagreement. The same woman who had written an article that upbraided judges for writing "separate opinions that generate more heat than light" had also celebrated in the same article the diversity of American opinions. Frequently, Ginsburg explained, foreign observers of our courts are "impressed, touched with envy or admiration, that our system of justice is so secure, we can tolerate open displays of disagreement among judges about what the law is."

It was also hard for others to second-guess Justice Ginsburg because of her refusal to play politics with cases. Stubbornly oblivious to what was popular, she refrained from making alliances and trading her vote on one case for someone else's in another. During a lecture in New York, Justice Ginsburg was asked by a student, "How do you stay committed to a position knowing that without political tradeoffs, your positions could be ignored given the conservative leanings of the Court?" She bluntly replied, "I believe firmly in what the Chief Justice says: 'The day a judge votes the way the home crowd wants is the day that person should step down from the bench.'"

Since becoming a Supreme Court justice, Ginsburg has had to cope with a great deal of attention directed toward her conduct, her writing, and even her appearance. Observers found her far more active than most junior justices. For example, Clarence Thomas, the justice appointed before Ginsburg, seldom spoke when he first started. Like her friend and fellow justice Antonin Scalia, Justice Ginsburg is known to be persistent in asking attorneys questions, posing as many as 17 questions in one hour.

Ginsburg is never intemperate or argumentative, however. "She goes to the heart of the issue," wrote one reporter. "Her questions are designed to get an answer while Scalia wants to 'catch' the lawyer in a contradiction."

About writing, Ginsburg has advised, "Get it right; keep it tight." Maria Simon, one of Justice Ginsburg's law clerks, remembers Ginsburg teaching the staff to write with "fewer words" and with "clear, crisp language." The justice has confessed that "sometimes, to be accurate is to be boring." Observers also note that there is no invective against others in her demeanor.

One reason for her plain, comprehensible language is that Ginsburg has a wider audience in mind than just Court personnel and litigants. She wants the general public to be able to comprehend the issues and choices. As one law clerk noted:

> Justice Ginsburg wrote these statements [bench statements] in readily understandable terms, recognizing the unique opportunity to communicate the court's work to the public, those present in the courtroom, and those who would learn of the decision via the press corps seated on the side of the courtroom. Expanding her audience wider still, Justice Ginsburg included many public appearances in her already demanding schedule. She gave generously of her time to so many groups, including law school students, women's organizations, and legal groups of all types.

Justice Ginsburg's office is flooded with tons of letters, some from critics but most from fans. Martin penned an all-purpose humorous reply to some of the most-asked questions. Justice Ginsburg's secretaries vetoed Martin's reply, however. In fact, when writers ask for signed cards and pictures, Ginsburg readily complies, and always signs them herself. When asked if she ever dreamed in her youth of becoming a Supreme Court justice, her sober answer was, "I didn't even think I'd make a living as a lawyer."

Justice Ginsburg warmly greets Secretary of State Madeleine Albright (left), with whom she shares a common bond. Both were appointed by President Clinton to high offices. Albright is the first woman to serve as U.S. Secretary of State.

As for Ginsburg's personal appearance, she jokes good-naturedly that after her 60th birthday, she was not prepared to be noticed by the Style section of the *New York Times* or listed in *People* magazine among "the worst dressed."

Justice Ginsburg's style of dress is like her writing: simply no-nonsense, plain, well-fitting, and correct. Her hair is pulled back flat in a neat bun and she wears simple, round glasses. Like the outfit of a clergy person, her understated attire does not call attention to itself. Still, feminine touches are added here and there: earrings, a pin, pearls, or beads.

Her surroundings in the U.S. Supreme Court building also reflect the simplicity of her personal style. She has an office on the second floor, where there is more light. Her offices are open, airy, and quiet. In Justice Ginsburg's five-room suite—called the justice's "chambers"—she is assisted by a staff of four law clerks, two secretaries, and a chamber's aide. Her choice of these chambers seems particularly fitting: they had been previously occupied by Justice Thurgood Marshall, noted for his landmark opinions on civil rights.

Justice Ginsburg's chambers overlook a pleasant courtyard where, on sunny days, staff members gather for lunch or work outdoors on stone benches around patio tables. Feeling somewhat uncomfortable with the typical dark, heavy oak and leather furniture that looked decidedly male, Justice Ginsburg furnished her chambers in a more modern decor of chrome and glass. Volumes of law books line the shelves, and modern art graces the walls. Photographs of family decorate the office, and a large mahogany desk with brass trim accommodates piles of papers and office supplies.

One of Ginsburg's male law clerks was a father with primary responsibility for the care of a small child. Taking the opportunity to set an example, Justice

Ginsburg allowed the clerk to work on a flexible schedule. Letting the clerk make the necessary adjustments to coordinate with his schedule was a new and special accommodation in Supreme Court chambers.

Justice Ginsburg enjoys a personal relationship with her staff. On many occasions she has turned her

Lecturing and speaking engagements are part of Ruth Bader Ginsburg's schedule as a Supreme Court justice. She is always eager to share her views on the law.

chambers into scenes of informal and festive activities. In the fall of 1993, peanut-butter-and-jelly sandwiches were most probably served for the first time in the Supreme Court reception room when Ruth hosted her granddaughter's third-birthday party. Other celebrations were marked in the justice's offices—with "scrumptious cakes" baked by Martin—for holiday parties and birthday teas.

As she had done when she was a judge on the U.S. Court of Appeals, Ginsburg goes on outings with her law clerks. Maria Simon fondly remembers an excursion conducted by Ruth: "One afternoon, she spirited us away from the court to attend an opera [performance] of *Carmen* at the Kennedy Center."

An avid opera fan, Justice Ginsburg was not the least bit intimidated when she was invited to appear as an extra onstage during a Washington Opera production. Accompanied by Antonin Scalia, also an opera buff, Ginsburg was decked out in a full period costume, complete with a fan and white wig.

When seated on the bench, however, Justice Ginsburg is all business. Much of her work resembles the routine she followed during her earlier years on the D.C. circuit court: intense preparation for cases, hearing cases, writing, and circulating opinions. As the junior justice, Ginsburg was assigned the post of door-keeper and vote recorder during weekly meetings. With 1,600 petitions needing review, this was no small task. "My anxiety at taking notes approached the level I felt at Harvard for my first practice exam," she recalled.

During Justice Ginsburg's first year on the bench, she voted for women's rights, civil rights, and voting rights. On criminal law, her voting record was mixed. Her pattern was described as somewhat "independent" as she agreed alternatively with both liberal and conservative members of the Court. Whichever way she voted, however, she was well prepared for many

A supporter of opera and an enthusiastic fan, Ruth Bader Ginsburg had the pleasure of actually dressing up, along with her colleague Antonin Scalia, to appear briefly onstage at the Washington Opera.

aspects of her new position.

Justice Ginsburg was quite familiar with issues of discrimination and most anxious to hear those cases. During her first term, she had the opportunity to decide that jurors could not be eliminated from juries solely on the basis of gender. She also had the opportunity to render a decision on an especially important case of sex discrimination. The case involved the admissions policy of the Virginia Military Institute (VMI), an all-male military college.

Founded in 1839, VMI was the last of Virginia's 15 public institutions of higher learning that admitted only men. The Supreme Court found that barring women from admission violated the equal protection clause of the Fourteenth Amendment. As a public institution that accepted state funds, the school could not exclude women from enrollment, particularly when national service academies such as West Point and the U.S. Naval Academy had been accepting women for several years. The Court also noted VMI's history of discrimination against African Americans and rejected the school's plan for a "separate but equal" facility for women at Mary Baldwin College. As was the case in instances of racial segregation, the Supreme Court said that two separate institutions were not equal in nature or quality.

In the Supreme Court's majority opinion, written by Justice Ginsburg, she stated, "The United States maintains that the Constitution's equal protection guarantee precludes Virginia from reserving exclusively to men the unique education opportunities VMI affords. We agree." She noted that similar objections had been made in the past about allowing women into law and medical schools. Ginsburg pointed out that although all female students might not be interested in the spartan training VMI offered, all men certainly did not find it appealing either.

Justice Ginsburg also emphasized that VMI had produced many distinguished leaders in politics, business, and the military. In denying women admission, VMI was preserving the school's advantages and opportunities exclusively for men. She concluded by writing: "Inherent differences between men and women, we have come to appreciate, remain cause for celebration, but not for denigration of the members of either sex or for artificial constraints on an individual's opportunity." She added, "Such classifications may not be used, as they once were . . . to create or perpetuate the legal, social, and economic inferiority of women."

Ginsburg dealt with areas outside sex discrimination, too. In one decision involving a financial issue, the Court reversed a plaintiff's criminal conviction for trying to avoid the federal requirement that banks report deposits of sums more than $10,000. Justice Ginsburg wrote the Court's opinion. Ever practical, she listed a number of innocent reasons why citizens might split up cash deposits into small sums.

Despite her reputation and exposure to the media, Ginsburg found that some who appeared before the Court still could not distinguish one woman from the other. She was referring to her colleague Sandra Day O'Connor. Appointed in 1981 by President Ronald Reagan, O'Connor was the first woman to serve on the Supreme Court. Even though the two women look nothing alike, many people tend to confuse them. "Just last term," wrote Ginsburg in 1997, "our Acting Solicitor General three times called me Justice O'Connor, and the same slip was made by a distinguished advocate, Harvard Law School Professor Lawrence Tribe."

Apparently anticipating this problem, one month after Ginsburg's appointment the National Association of Women Judges gave the two women justices custom-printed T-shirts. On the back of both shirts appear the words "The Supremes." The front of one T-shirt says, "I am Sandra, not Ruth"; the other reads, "I am Ruth, not Sandra."

An important difference between the Supreme Court and the appellate courts is the number of judges who sit together on each case. Reaching agreement among nine judges is more difficult than doing so with a panel of three judges. Justice Ginsburg speaks often

Since some people who appeared before the Supreme Court had difficulty distinguishing between Ruth Bader Ginsburg and her colleague Sandra Day O'Connor (far right), the two justices were presented with identifying T-shirts, which unfortunately they couldn't wear on the bench.

of the respect the justices show for one another and their spirit of working together, which she considers more pronounced than that found at any other post she has held. It is the responsibility of the high court to interpret the Constitution, which Justice Ginsburg considers a living, "evolving document." In writing about the Constitution and its impact on the lives of all Americans, she has noted that when the nation's founders spoke of "we the people," not everyone was included:

Qualified voters when the nation was new bore more than a passing resemblance to the framers: the franchise was confined to property-owning adult white males, people free from dependence on others and therefore considered trustworthy citizens, not susceptible to influence or control by masters, overlords, or supervisors. In 1787, only five of the thirteen states had abolished slavery, women did not count as part of the franchise-holding, politically active community in any state, and wealth qualifications severely limited voter eligibility even among white males.

Given this limitation, Justice Ruth Bader Ginsburg is ever mindful of the need to preserve the spirit rather than the letter of the founding fathers' intent.

Smiling and relaxed, Ruth Bader Ginsburg reflects the mood of a woman who has fulfilled all of her personal and professional dreams.

8

FULFILLING
HER DESTINY

One of the duties Ruth Bader Ginsburg can perform as a judge and Justice is conducting marriage ceremonies. Son James recalls, "My mother went into the wedding business— she sometimes shared officiating with a rabbi." One of the most recent weddings Justice Ginsburg performed took place on January 17, 1999. She officiated at the marriage of James's cousin Mindy, daughter of Martin's younger brother, Bob. Her most memorable wedding, however, was that of James and his bride, Lisa Brauston, on November 17, 1995. James, who records music under the Cedille label, had met Lisa, an art historian, five years earlier.

Justice Ginsburg began this very special ceremony with introductory remarks: "When James and Lisa asked me to officiate at this wedding ceremony, I was at once pleased and concerned— pleased that they would want me to preside as we witness their declarations and exchange of vows; concerned that I could manage my part with no tears. But if there are tears, James and Lisa, they will be for your happiness."

Ruth Bader Ginsburg is surrounded by her family after performing the marriage ceremony for son James (center) and his bride, Lisa. Daughter Jane (far left) and Jane's children were there for the celebration.

She then spoke personally of the changes love brought into James's life. Her thoughts echoed the family's bonds and Ruth and Martin's view of their own marriage:

When Lisa became James's dearest friend, I told her of a change I had seen in my son. Lovable as he is, he is also challenging. Like his parents and sister, he is strong-willed. . . . The change was simply this: since Lisa came into James's life, he has seemed to be more satisfied with himself, more content with his work and days, more eager to pursue the joy and music of being alive. May Lisa's bright spirit and uncommon caring, and James's appreciation of her, ever make of the two magically more—wiser, richer in experience, happier—than either could be alone.

James and Lisa come to this wedding day with affection, respect, and understanding for each other. They embark on a partnership in life without reservation, and with love that provides shelter from fear, and the basis for hope, courage, and fulfillment. A marriage unites two individuals, and it also brings together two families.

Ruth and Martin have expressed great pride in both of their children and have actively supported each of them in the careers of their choosing. James describes himself as more like his father than his mother in terms of his sense of humor and old-fashioned ways. James explains that "Lisa says I even talk like Dad using outdated words such as 'ice-box' and 'valise.'"

In appearance, Jane also resembles her father. Jane's career, however, is more like that of her mother. Ruth and Jane were the first mother-daughter pair to attend Harvard Law School, where both worked on the *Harvard Law Review*. Jane, like Ruth, also became a professor at Columbia Law School. In addition, each woman has two children, a boy and a girl. (Jane's second child, Clara Simone Spera, had been born in 1990.)

Three years after their marriage, James and Lisa became the proud parents of Miranda Erin Ginsburg, born on April 30, 1998, in Chicago. The grandchildren call Ruth "Bubbie," the traditional Yiddish word for grandmother. As being a mother was extremely important to Ruth, so too is being a grandmother. When speaking of the central aspects of identity and experience she brings to her work at the Supreme Court, Justice Ginsburg lists "being a women, being a Jew, and being a parent."

In addition to being a parent and a justice, Ruth Bader Ginsburg continues her other career as a teacher and speaker, visiting a variety of places in the United States and abroad. During the summer of 1993, her first year on the Supreme Court, she taught at New York University. That same year, she was also honored with the Margaret Brent Women Lawyers of Achievement Award by the American Bar Association Commission on Women in the Profession.

In 1994 Justices Ginsburg and Scalia traveled to India where they lectured to judges and lawyers. That same year found Ginsburg at the Valparaiso Law School of Cambridge University in England. The following year, she visited both Jerusalem and Tel Aviv in Israel for a series of lectures and a conference on international human rights.

From 1996 through 1998, Ginsburg kept up her typical hectic schedule, teaching at schools in France, Spain, and Austria. In the summer of 1998, she and three Supreme Court colleagues met with judges in Luxembourg, Belgium, Germany, and France.

In the summer of 1999, Ruth and Martin Ginsburg taught on the Greek island of Crete as part of the law faculty of Louisiana's Tulane University. While in Greece, Ruth developed severe abdominal pain. Doctors at first thought she had a disorder of the large intestine, but the pain was actually unrelated to the colon cancer diagnosed in mid-September.

Justice Ginsburg was admitted to Washington Hospital Center in Washington, D.C., where on September 17 she underwent surgery. The surgeons removed her sigmoid colon—the lower third of her large intestine— and a small cancerous tumor along with it. Doctors said that tests showed no evidence that the disease had spread to the lymph nodes or to any organs.

"The justice is very lucky to have had this picked up incidently," said Dr. Harmon Eyre, chief medical officer for the American Cancer Society in Atlanta,

Georgia. "If it had been left alone it would have advanced to another stage."

Despite her 11-day hospital stay and required rest-and-recuperation period, Ginsburg continued to participate in the Court's ongoing work and on October 5, when the 1999 Supreme Court session opened, Justice Ruth Bader Ginsburg was present. One month later she reported that she was still "a little wobbly," and went on to say "but I progress steadily."

Later in October, Ginsburg spoke to the International

Justice Ginsburg receives mail from admirers as well as critics from across the nation. She cannot answer every letter, but she gladly fulfills requests for pictures and cards and signs them herself.

Women's Forum, an organization of female leaders from around the world. "When I accepted the invitation to be with you at this conference, I did not know how thankful I would be just to be here," said Ginsburg to loud applause from the audience.

When President Clinton sought a person "with heart" as well as experience and intellect, he chose a woman who can help guide the Supreme Court into the new millennium. Some people forget that wisdom is far more important than an outstanding résumé. In Ruth Bader Ginsburg, America gained a jurist whose concept of law and justice includes all the nation's citizens, great and small. Along with eight other justices, Justice Ginsburg will help interpret the Constitution for a new century.

1933   Ruth Joan Bader born to Celia Amster Bader and Nathan Bader on March 15 in Belle Harbor, New York

1935   Family moves to Flatbush section of Brooklyn, New York; older sister, Marilyn, dies of meningitis at age eight

1938   Enters Public School 238 in Brooklyn

1946   Enters James Madison High School; belongs to Arista honor society

1950   Mother dies of cancer at age 47; graduates from James Madison High School; enters Cornell University; meets Martin David Ginsburg

1953   Becomes engaged to Martin Ginsburg

1954   Graduates from Cornell University; marries Martin Ginsburg on June 23

1955   Moves to Fort Sill, Oklahoma, where Martin serves in the army; works for local Social Security office; daughter Jane Carol born on July 21

1956   Enters Harvard University Law School, one of nine female students in a class of more than 500

1957   Elected to *Harvard Law Review*; Martin diagnosed with cancer

1958   Martin recovers and graduates from law school; family moves to New York City where Martin enters law firm; Ruth transfers to Columbia University Law School, one of 12 female students in the school

1959   Elected to *Columbia Law Review;* named a Kent Scholar; graduates from Columbia; admitted to the New York bar; begins working as a law clerk at the U.S. District Court for the Southern District of New York

1962   Works in Sweden as a research associate for Columbia Law School Project on International Procedure

1963   Becomes associate director of Project on International Procedure; accepts assistant professorship at Rutgers University School of Law in Newark, New Jersey

1965   Son James Steven born on September 8; publishes first book, *Civil Procedure in Sweden*, coauthored with Anders Bruzelius

1966   Receives promotion to associate professor at Rutgers; serves on the Foreign Law Committee of the Association of the Bar of the City of New York; serves on the editorial board of the *American Journal of Comparative Law*

CHRONOLOGY

1967   Becomes a member of the European Law Committee of the American Bar Association (ABA)

1968   Publishes second book, *Swedish Code of Judicial Procedure;* becomes member of the Citizens Union; father dies

1969   Receives full professorship at Rutgers; edits *Business Regulation in the Common Market Nations*

1971   Principal writer of brief for sex-discrimination case brought before the Supreme Court; helps found the Women's Rights Project of the American Civil Liberties Union (ACLU)

1972   Accepts full professorship at Columbia Law School

1973   Presents first oral argument before Supreme Court; becomes the general counsel of the ACLU

1975   Wins Supreme Court decision in sex-discrimination case involving issue of Social Security benefits; admitted to the District of Columbia Bar; teaches in Holland and France

1977   Argues and wins second case involving Social Security before the Supreme Court; becomes a fellow at Stanford University's Center for Advanced Study in the Behavioral Sciences

1978   Becomes a council member of the American Law Institute and a fellow of the American Bar Foundation; visits China with a select group from the ABA

1979   Receives Outstanding Teacher of Law Award from the Society of American Law Teachers

1980   Accepts appointment by President Jimmy Carter as a federal judge on U.S. Court of Appeals for the District of Columbia Circuit; moves to Washington, D.C.; receives Barnard College Woman of Achievement Award; joins the Women's Bar Association of the District of Columbia; Martin begins teaching law at Georgetown University in Washington, D.C.

1982   Elected a fellow at the American Academy of Arts and Sciences; becomes a member of the National Association of Women Judges

1985   Begins serving as an adviser for the American Law Institute's Project on Complex Litigation

1986   Grandson Paul Bertrand Spera born; Ruth becomes a member of the Federal Judges Association

1987   Husband, Martin Ginsburg, undergoes triple bypass heart surgery

1988   Becomes a member of the U.S. Judicial Conference Committee for the Fifth International Appellate Judges Conference

1990   Granddaughter Clara Simone Spera born October 3

1993   Accepts nomination as associate justice of the Supreme Court on June 14; nomination confirmed by Senate in July; takes the oath of office as Supreme Court justice on August 10; receives the Margaret Brent Women Lawyers of Achievement Award from the American Bar Association Commission on Women in the Profession

1994   Rules with other justices in favor of the National Organization for Women (NOW) against antiabortion protesters; travels to India with Justice Antonin Scalia and delivers lectures

1995   Travels to Jerusalem and Tel Aviv for lectures and a conference on constitutional law; performs wedding ceremony for son James and Lisa Brauston on November 17

1998   Granddaughter Miranda Erin Ginsburg born April 30; travels to Europe during summer

1999   Visits Greek island of Crete with Martin during summer to teach a program sponsored by Tulane University; falls ill and is later diagnosed with colon cancer; undergoes cancer surgery in Washington, D.C., recovers and returns to work for October 5 opening of 1999 Supreme Court session

BIBLIOGRAPHY

Ayer, Elinor H. *Ruth Bader Ginsburg: Fire and Steel on the Supreme Court.* New York: Dillon Press, 1994.

Bayer, Linda. "Supreme Court to Get Most Modern *Bubbie.*" *Washington Jewish Week* and *Kansas City Chronicle*, 24 June 1993.

Carlson, Margaret. "The Law According to Ruth." *Time*, 28 June 1993.

Deibel, Mary. "Senate's Spotlight on Ginsburg." *Rocky Mountain News*, 19 July 1993.

Friedman, Jeanette. "Ruth Bader Ginsburg: A Rare Interview." *Lifestyles*, March, 1994.

Gilbert, Lynn and Gaylen Moore. *Particular Passions: Talks with Women Who Have Shaped Our Times.* New York: Crown Books, 1981.

Ginsburg, Ruth Bader. *Jewish Supreme Court Justices.* Delivered in Washington, D.C. *B'Nai B'rith International,* 1 September 1996.

Ginsburg, Ruth Bader. *Reflections of Justice Ginsburg.* Lansing, Mich.: 1995.

Hewitt, Bill. "Feeling Supreme." *People*, 28 June 1993.

Huber, Peter W. *Sandra Day O'Connor.* New York: Chelsea House, 1990.

Italia, Bob. *Ruth Bader Ginsburg: United States Supreme Court Library.* Minneapolis, Minn.: Abdo & Daughters, 1994.

Kaplan, David. "Take Down the Girlie Calendars." *Newsweek*, 22 November 1993.

Kaplan, David and Bob Cohn. "A Frankfurter, Not a Hotdog." *Newsweek,* 28 June 1993.

Kaus, Mickey. "Roe to Ruin." *The New Republic*, 12 April 1993.

Roberts, Jack L. *Ruth Bader Ginsburg, Supreme Court Justice.* Brookfield, Conn.: Millbrook Press, 1994.

Roberts, Steven. "Two Lives of Ruth Bader Ginsburg." *U.S. News and World Report*, 28 June 1993.

Saline, Carol and Sharon Wohlmuth. *Mothers and Daughters.* New York: Doubleday, 1997.

Swiger, Elinor Porter. *Women Lawyers at Work.* New York: Julian Messner, 1978.

Van Geel, T. R. *Understanding the Supreme Court.* New York: University of Rochester, 1997.

INDEX

PICTURE CREDITS

Linda Bayer has an M.A. in psychology and studied for an Ed.D. at the Graduate School of Education at Harvard University. She also has an M.A. in English and a Ph.D. in humanities. Dr. Bayer has worked with patients suffering from substance abuse and other problems at Judge Baker Guidance Center and within the Boston public school system. She served on the faculties of several universities, including Boston University and the Hebrew University in Israel, where she occupied the Sam and Ayala Zacks Chair and was twice a writer in residence in Jerusalem.

Dr. Bayer was a newspaper editor and syndicated columnist, winning the Simon Rockower Award for excellence in journalism. She is the author of hundreds of articles and is working on her 15th book. She has written for a number of public figures, including General Colin Powell and President Bill Clinton. She is currently a senior writer and strategic analyst at the White House.

Dr. Bayer is the mother of two children, Lev and Ilana.

Elaine Andrews (contributing editor) is a writer and editor of educational materials for children and young adults and the author of two nonfiction books for young readers.

Matina S. Horner was president of Radcliffe College and associate professor of psychology and social relations at Harvard University. She is best known for her studies of women's motivation, achievement, and personality development. Dr. Horner has served on several national boards and advisory councils, including those of the National Science Foundation, Time Inc., and the Women's Research and Education Institute. She earned her B.A. from Bryn Mawr College and her Ph.D. from the University of Michigan, and holds honorary degrees from many colleges and universities, including Mount Holyoke, Smith, Tufts, and the University of Pennsylvania.

ACKNOWLEDGMENTS

The author wishes to thank Ruth Bader Ginsburg for the lengthy exclusive interview she granted on March 18, 1999. Much appreciation is also extended to Martin Ginsburg for two in-depth interviews. Thanks also to James Steven Ginsburg and Jane Ginsburg Spera for the generous interviews they gave.

The author would also like to thank a host of Ginsburg friends and relatives who kindly shared their time, memories, photographs, and biographical materials. Special thanks to the following people: Judge Richard Salzman of Washington, D.C.; Jane Gervitz, Justice Ginsburg's cousin; Ruth and Melvin Wortman, current owners of Camp Che-Na-Wah; Harryette Gordon Helsel, a close high school friend of Justice Ginsburg; and Ann Burkhardt Kittner, another good friend of Justice Ginsburg.